SLATS
GROBNIK
AND
SOME
OTHER
FRIENDS

BOOKS BY MIKE ROYKO

Up Against It

I May Be Wrong, But I Doubt It

Boss: Richard J. Daley of Chicago

Slats Grobnik and Some Other Friends

E. P. DUTTON & CO., INC. · NEW YORK · 1973

SLATS
GROBNIK
AND
SOME
OTHER
FRIENDS

Columns: 1966-1973

by

MIKE
ROYKO

For
Daryle
Feldmeir

SLATS
GROBNIK

SEASON ARRIVES FOR THE OLDEST PROTEST OF ALL

September 7, 1966

Those back-to-school memories return every year at this time.

The sights are all around us. Eager, scrubbed young faces. Well-stocked school supplies stores. Patrol boys. School windows, yet unbroken.

What an exciting day it always was, that first day back. The fun of seeing the other kids, after a long summer, the anticipation of meeting a new teacher, the challenge of tackling new studies.

It seems like only yesterday morning that . . .

"Get up. It's after 7."

"Oooooooohhhh."

3

"What's wong?"

"I'm sick."

"Where?"

"I got a sore throat."

"Let me look. . . . It looks fine to me. Get up."

"I just can't go to school today. Please, lemme stay home."

"Why?"

"Slats Grobnik said he'd beat me up next time he saw me."

"When did he say that?"

"The last day of school. That's why I stayed in all summer."

"Tell him if he hits you you'll tell your father."

"I did. Slats said he'd beat him up, too."

"That's ridiculous."

"Oh yeah? Slats is bigger than the school janitor. He even got more tattoos than the janitor."

"Well, if he hits you, tell the teacher."

"Her? Mrs. Primprim? A lot she cares. She hates me. She's the meanest, lousiest . . ."

"Watch your language."

"Whah? I didn't swear."

"Don't forget to put on clean socks."

"What for? We don't have gym the first day."

"I don't know why you always act this way. Don't you want to see your friends?"

"Aaagghhhh!"

"What about that nice boy, Archie?"

"Him? He eats paste, the pig."

"What about Jenny, the girl from the next block? I thought you liked her."

"Aagghh. She never blows her nose."

"Well, just remember to stay away from Stanley."

"Whah? He's my best friend."

"Never mind. He's always got nits in his hair and you'll catch . . ."

"My best friend and I can't even . . . boy!"

"Eat your breakfast before it gets cold."

"I don't care. Hey, I just remembered. School don't start until tomorrow. Yeah, I heard that on the radio."

"Then what are those patrol boys doing on the corner?"

"I dunno. Practicing or something."

"That's enough. You're going to school today."

"Boy! Then you got to give me money for school supplies."

"Get me my purse. How much?"

"Fourteen or fifteen dollars."

"What?"

"Well, we got to buy a lot of new notebooks and paper and. . . ."

"Here's 50 cents."

"Awright for you. If I flunk it'll be your fault."

"Hurry, it's getting late."

"What about my lunch money?"

"Come home for lunch."

"Aw, lemme eat at the school store today. All the guys. . . ."

"What can you get there?"

"A Twinkie. Cream soda. Lots of stuff."

"You come home for lunch. I'll make soup."

"Soup. I never have no fun."

"Here's your jacket. It's chilly outside."

"Aww, nobody else'll be wearing a jacket. They'll all look at me. . . ."

"Wear your jacket. And pull the collar up; your neck is dirty."

"Boy!"

"Sometimes I just don't understand."

"Whah? Whah?"

"How you ever got into college?"

"You know—the GI bill."

WHATTA FIND: A LIVE PINBOY!

The creature you see below is widely believed to be extinct. He is the Bowling Alley Pinboy.

I am happy to report that he still exists. The picture was taken a couple of days ago when I found the Pinboy thriving in his natural habitat, the back of a bowling alley.

This is a discovery of which I am proud. I feel like one of those scientists who creep around a swamp for years and then spot a rare bird.

Those who doubt the picture's authenticity can verify the existence of the pinboy at Chicago Recreation, an old-fashioned eight-alley bowling hall on the second floor at 3039 W. 26th St.

It could be the last commercial alley in town that is not au-

6

tomated. A few manual racks exist in church halls, I'm told, but they don't count because a place isn't a bowling alley if it doesn't sell beer.

George Melka, bartender and manager of Chicago Recreation, says automation passed his place because it is so small. The automators were busy installing their machines in the huge, super, family emporiums that have sprung up.

"We don't mind," Melka says. "In fact, we're kind of proud of it. People come in here sometimes and look surprised like you did. Especially the guys who used to set pins themselves.

"I personally think pinboys are faster than machines. How about it, Tom? Don't you think you're faster?"

Tom, a lean, white-haired man of about 50, was studying the race results. "I dunno," he shrugged. He wore baggy pants, a sweat shirt, gym shoes and an old Army fatigue cap. "I dunno. Maybe I am, maybe I ain't. But if I make a mistake, you don't have to call in an engineer."

Four teen-agers came in and asked for an alley. Tom looked them over, decided they knew how to bowl, and walked back to set pins for them.

That's really why automation had to come to bowling. Most teen-agers prefer to knock pins down rather than set them up. And their fathers, probably former pinsetters, provide the money.

But not many years ago, thousands of kids (that's what we were called) made spending money by setting pins. Plus a lot of dropouts, drifters, winos and moonlighters.

The pay rate, as I recall, was about 7 or 8 cents a game. So if you set "double" (adjoining alleys) for two leagues, you worked 60 games in about four or five hours and earned $4.80, plus maybe 50 cents or a dollar in tips. (Tom gets 15 cents a line, or $8, for two leagues.)

Pinsetting was also a fine physical fitness program. To earn the $4.80, you bent over about 2,000 times. There weren't many fat pinboys.

I don't know what the labor laws were, but many of us started setting pins when we were about 12. You could tell a pinboy by the joints on his first two fingers. Hoisting the pins between the fingers made them big.

By the time Slats Grobnik was 15, the joints on his fingers were bigger than his brain.

Slats was the last pinsetter I ever saw, except me. He knew all the tricks, such as how to get revenge on drunks who threw balls while you were bending over for the pins.

The drunks never knew it, but Slats would put different substances in the ball's holes before he returned it—things too terrible to mention here.

When he had to set pins for girls, which was very slow and unprofitable work because they did not bowl well, Slats always speeded things by keeping a couple of the rear pins out of the rack. Or he'd kick over a corner pin if it would make a strike. And if he really liked a girl, he'd shout something dirty to show how he felt.

Slats' pinboy career ended, though, because of an ape. That is what we called the big goofs who couldn't bowl well but zinged the ball as hard as they could. It made the pins fly and an ape was happiest when a pin boy got hit.

Slats was hit in the head and it improved his IQ so much that he became the foul line spotter. Before the electric eye, this was a good job. You sat in a roost and watched the foul line. When a toe crossed it, you pushed the button for that alley and foul light went on.

It was more power than Slats ever had in his life and he was ruthless. He'd sit up there banging on the foul buttons like he was Cornel Wilde playing Chopin.

He held the job until one night he called two straight fouls on a bowler from the transformer department of a factory league.

The bowler called Slats a filthy name but Slats came back with a better one.

When the bowler charged at Slats' roost, Slats, no coward, jumped down, fists ready.

She flattened him with one punch and Slats never got over it. He never went back to the foul line even though we kept telling him that she was a lot bigger so he shouldn't feel bad.

A
SLICK
DREAM
WITH
LOOPHOLES

Things like this usually don't anger me, but enough is enough.

Every year, at about this time, the nation's slick magazines come out with big stories about the new bathing-suit fashions for the summer.

Basically, the message is always the same: The suits will be even skimpier, more daring, more revealing, more shocking. Parts of the anatomy that have never before been exposed to the light of a day will peel.

The magazines are on the newsstands and this year's bathing suit stories are in them. The suits are going to be skimpier, more shocking, revealing, daring.

And if the suits aren't skimpier, at least the cloth has been shifted around.

On the cover of McCall's is a girl who has on a couple of pieces of cloth. Her hair is blowing in her face, which makes her face the best-concealed part of the picture.

Time magazine has 12 girls spread across six of its little pages.

Some are wearing see-through crocheted suits. Another has on three dabs held together by strips of clear vinyl.

A long blond has a yellow two-piece suit connected by a gold link chain.

Time says the chain "is anything but déjà vu."

I don't even know what "déjà vu" means, but when a writer is afraid to say something in English, that's always a tipoff that it's pretty wild.

There's an American Indian-style loincloth bikini, designed by that old Western folklorist, Emilio Pucci. I don't believe Indian girls ever dressed that way. There wouldn't have been all that fighting over land if they had.

It's not the scanty bathing suits that bother me. I don't care if girls want to run around the beach that way. It's their sunburn.

But the thing that bothers me is that it is all a lie.

Girls never wear those kinds of suits. At least not around here.

I know, because whenever the new fashions are announced, I get down to the beach to see if they are wearing them. So I can write a story, naturally.

I hoof up and down the shoreline. I sit for hours on a bench. Sometimes, for a better view, I crawl up in a tree and sit there. Once in a while a friend lets me use his high-rise apartment and I spend days scanning the lakefront with binoculars.

I don't care what Emilio Pucci and Time magazine say. The girls don't wear things that are "anything but déjà vu." They wear the same kinds of bathing suits they've been wearing for years.

The big furor about topless bathing suits was an example.

All the magazines had stories when a designer named Rudi Gernreich said topless suits were the coming style.

Naturally, I went to the beach and waited.

Slats Grobnik went with me because Slats, in a way, was the originator of the idea.

Years ago, when we were young men, the whole gang would sit around the beach and every time a good-looking girl walked by, Slats yelled something that was basically what Rudi Gernreich had in mind.

But nobody ever gave Slats credit for being years ahead of the times in fashion ideas. They just said he was a disgusting creep.

So when the topless suits were announced, we spent days around the beaches. Slats had more cameras around his neck than a combat correspondent. We sat on one beach for so long, just doing nothing but staring, that somebody put us on a city payroll.

Nothing. The only excitement was when Slats jumped up and started whistling and cheering and pointing at somebody coming out of the beach house. Slats is nearsighted. It turned out to be a real flabby guy. Once again everybody said Slats was a disgusting creep.

All we got out of that summer—and the other summers since—were sunburned noses.

And this year there won't be any see-through crocheted suits. Or suits with a chain that "is anything but déjà vu."

But I've wised up, at last. This year we won't get sunburned noses. We'll sit in the shade.

GROBNIK'S END
AN EYE-OPENER

June 26, 1968

The United States Supreme Court ruled last week that getting drunk in public is a crime.

Of course it is. Anybody could have told them that. When something carries such severe punishment, it has to be a crime.

As Slats Grobnik's old man used to say, after his wife finished with him: "You'd think I killed somebody."

Mr. Grobnik knew more about the subject of public drunkenness than anybody on the Supreme Court, and he never even went to law school.

He used to get drunk in public pretty often. Once a day, at least.

In the winter, his favorite public place was the inside of the corner tavern. In summer, he preferred a chair outside the front door of the tavern. He said he sat out there because fresh air was essential for a long life.

Had he done his drinking at home, it wouldn't have been a crime because it is not unlawful to be drunk in private.

But if he could have done his drinking at home, he wouldn't have been drunk in the first place.

When he first married, he used to keep a bottle under the sink and would have a few drinks after work.

Today, this is known as gracious living, especially if the shots are mixed with ice.

But after Slats and his brother Fats were born, Mrs. Grobnik told old man Grobnik that he couldn't drink at home anymore.

She said it would be a bad influence on the children. "If they see you drinking at home, they'll grow up to be bums." She read this in the Reader's Digest.

Old man Grobnik argued that they would probably grow up to be bums, anyway.

But she wouldn't give in. One day, she emptied a full bottle in the sink. He walked out for good, but he came back when the precinct captain's brother, who was a lawyer, told him that as bad a thing as she had done, he would still have to pay alimony.

That's when he started committing the crime of being drunk in public.

At first, it was just a few drinks. But when he came home she yelled about it.

So in order to withstand the yelling, he increased the dosage. Then she berated him even more. And he would drink more. The escalation went out of control.

That's the way it went for 25 years.

I later calculated that Mrs. Grobnik yelled at old man Grobnik for about two hours a day during all those years.

That means he spent one year and 11 months of his life being yelled at.

Financiers embezzle money on Wall Street and judges give them probation. Rich doctors cheat on their income tax and get off with a fine.

But for getting drunk in public, old man Grobnik spent one year and 11 months being yelled at.

If a burglar gets a year and 11 months in jail, at least it's quiet.

But in the end, old man Grobnik got the last word.

One night, he fell off the chair in front of the tavern and hit his head. He had lost his balance while reaching out to pinch a passing lady.

His eyes were closed when some members of the Armittage Av. Athletic and Social Club carried him into the parlor. The doctor said they would never open again.

But they did, one more time. And he just smiled and nodded at Slats and Fats.

Then he looked at Mrs. Grobnik and shrugged:

"See? I told you they'd grow up to be bums anyway."

HE
CAN
DREAM,
CAN'T
HE?

It was early last Thursday morning and I heard a strange sound. It was Slats Grobnik's voice. He was in front of the house yelling: "Yo, ho, ho . . . can you come out?"

He was on the sidewalk and he had a big, brown paper bag in his arms. He pointed at it with one finger.

We met in the gangway a few minutes later.

He opened the bag. "Lookit," he hissed.

"Wow," I hissed.

There were Zebras by the package, and cherry bombs, torpedoes and skyrockets, more Zebras, pinwheels and other great stuff.

"Wherejagettum," I hissed.

16

"Gynatruck cameroun' sellnum," he hissed.

"Boy," I hissed.

"Let's go," he hissed, and we trotted quietly out of the gangway and into the alley.

He found an empty soup can.

Then he took a thick, stubby cherry bomb out of the bag and placed it on the ground. He put the can over it so just the wick stuck out.

He lit a punk with a match, then touched the punk to the cherry bomb wick. And jumped back.

The sound bounced off the garages and the houses. It rattled windows and shook porches. Mortar trickled from between bricks. Cats fled.

The can leaped at the sky, climbing higher than the garages, above the power lines, beyond the rooftops, almost disappearing in the clouds.

Then it fell slowly, clattering on the pavement.

Slats picked it up. The unopened end was puffed out, the inside scorched by the force of the explosion.

"Lookit," he hissed.

"Boy," I hissed.

"Let's try it with a coffee can," he hissed. We blew up the coffee can. Then we shot up two juice cans at the same time.

Somebody came out on a back porch and shook his fist.

We tossed a Zebra firecracker into his yard, then turned and trotted quietly up the alley and into the street.

As we trotted, we tossed torpedoes against the brick walls of buildings, leaving a wave of explosions behind us.

"Torpedoes are just as loud as cherry bombs," I shouted.

"No they're not," Slats shouted.

"Well, they're as loud as Zebras," I shouted.

"Yeah," he shouted, banging one against the candy store wall.

"Don't waste 'em," Slats yelled, lighting one whole package of Zebras and tossing it on Mr. Yoboff's porch.

"I won't," I yelled, dropping one whole package of Zebras into Mr. Lynch's mailbox.

"They got to last all day," Slats bellowed, laying out a row of torpedoes on the streetcar tracks.

"I know," I bellowed, aiming a barrage of rockets at the school windows.

We trotted down the street, as the streetcar set off a chain of explosions and Lynch's mailbox sailed into the yard and Mr. Yoboff's porch trembled and three of six school windows suffered direct hits.

"This is more fun than I've had in years," Slats howled.

"Me, too," I howled.

Everybody was outside, shaking their fists.

We trotted faster. At the end of the street, on the corner, all the guys were waiting. They all had big, brown paper bags.

We trotted faster. But we didn't get any closer. All the guys started fading away, disappearing. And Slats started disappearing.

It was last Thursday morning and I was awakened by a strange sound. It was the alarm clock. I listened for the "yo ho, ho, can you come out?" Nothing.

Ahhh, nuts.

THE
ACCORDION
vs.

THE
GUITAR

_____

July 31, 1968

_____

The accordion is said to be slipping out of sight as a popular instrument.

Since 1950, when 130,000 were sold, it has dropped to a recent one-year sale of 35,000.

Guitars, meanwhile, are being sold by the millions.

There was a time when, in my neighborhood alone, there must have been 35,000 accordions. The only guitar player was a hillbilly who always strummed sad songs because hard times had forced him to leave his native Wilson Av. and live with people who used garlic.

There were a lot of reasons why the accordion was popular among the working and drinking classes.

It made a lot of noise for just one instrument. There was no future as a tavern or wedding virtuoso if you took up the flute or harp. You needed a big instrument that would drown out the sound of stomping feet, breaking glasses and falling bodies.

Also, the accordion looked something like the only other musical instrument people in the neighborhood were familiar with—the juke box. It gleamed and has as many colors as new kitchen linoleum.

Nobody saw sense in spending money on something like a violin, which was small, made of wood, and would break if you hit someone with it.

Some people, mostly girls, played the piano. But it never caught on big because you couldn't take it to a picnic.

One of the better accordion players I knew was Slats Grobnik.

Like others, he studied at Walter's Academy of Music, which was next to the Exterminating Store on Milwaukee Av.

Walter was the dean of the academy and was also famous for his Saturday night concerts at the Jump Rite Inn. He knew more dirty lyrics to "I Got A Girl Friend Her Name is Mary Polka" than any accordionist I ever heard.

Slats didn't want to play the accordion. He preferred the violin because it was small and he was lazy. But his mother said: "You can't play the violin. People will think we're Jewish."

"Besides," she said, "if you learn the accordion you can earn money playing on weekends at the taverns. And that will give you a chance to get to know your father."

This was not a minor investment, the accordion lessons. In the beginning, Walter loaned an accordion free and charged only for the lessons. But as soon as a kid remembered to take his finger out of his nose and press a key, Walter told the parents that the boy was a genius and should own his own instrument.

If a youth had talent, and was too dumb to conceal it, he would probably get an accordion with his initials on the front.

Then he was trapped, because it was hard to resell with initials.

As soon as his repertoire included one polka and a Hit Parade foxtrot he was dragged into the parlor and forced to perform for his aunts, uncles and snickering cousins.

Next it would be a picnic and the chance to show you could play with mosquitoes in your ears and somebody spilling beer on the keys.

Then on stage at the neighborhood movie house's Saturday Talent Show. It was a thrill to stand there with all your friends in the front row yelling that you stink.

For the very best, the big-time was going on Morris B. Sachs' Radio Amateur Hour, and playing "Lady of Spain I Adore You."

The biggest competition for first place was always an Irish tenor who sang the Lord's Prayer, and a girl tap dancer.

It wasn't hard to beat the girl tap dancer because when you heard one tap on the radio, you heard them all. But first prize always seemed to go to the Irish tenor who sang the Lord's Prayer. It was no surprise to our neighborhood when Morris B. Sachs went into politics.

It is to be expected that the accordion has given way to the guitar. That's the result of the nation's wealth and buying power shifting from the adult to the child.

With his own money, today's teen-ager can buy the instrument of his choice. If he has no money, he can still persuade his parents to give him a guitar by threatening to have a nervous breakdown or father a child.

The teen-ager selects the guitar because he is, basically, a slothful creature, easily offended by physical exertion. The accordion is a large instrument that requires a certain amount of heaving and sweating if it is to be played noisily.

The guitar, however, is a light instrument, easily carried by a teen-age girl, or even a teen-age boy. And you get a tremendous noise out of it, especially when it is combined with a youth who sings at the top of his adenoids about how his heart is broken because he and his love want to get married but nobody will buy them a car.

And that, in simple sociological terms, is why we have millions of little John Lennons making our music.

There is no reason to regret this, though. If the accordion had remained popular, the country would be overrun today by a horde of teen-age Lawrence Welks. And half the parents would be in hock paying for bubble machines.

AN
ARRESTING
JOB
PROBLEM

Most of the youths in my neighborhood had it drummed into their heads that just one arrest would result in a lifelong black mark that would make it impossible to get a job.

It became part of our street lore that even if we lied, an employer would somehow, some day find out and confront us with the evidence and a pink slip.

Even something as minor as filching Twinkies, breaking school windows, or shoplifting at the dime store would put anything more ambitious than being pinboys beyond our reach.

Mr. Grobnik was always telling his boy Slats: "Just one pinch, kid, and you'll never get no job."

Slats always answered: "That won't interfere with my plans." But he never got in trouble anyway because it would have kept him awake.

We never doubted that it was all true. And we were very careful about what we did. Not careful about staying out of trouble, but careful in planning what we did so we wouldn't get caught, which is the secret to success even today.

Now it appears that my generation was the last that worried about arrest records.

Today's young people, at least those active in the many forms of protest, are marching into the future with arrest records as long as their hair.

Some have been involved in protests for several years. They were arrested in the South for civil rights activity, in the North for antiwar protests, on campuses for almost anything and on the streets for just being around and having long hair when the wagon arrived.

It's impossible to tell how many college-educated, middle class youths have established records since it all began. But it surely numbers well into the thousands. Several hundred were arrested during the Democratic convention alone.

So the best educated, best fed generation of middle-class youths in our history is probably going to have the most impressive arrest record.

This will eventually cause a problem that most personnel directors have never thought about.

What do you do about the young man or woman with a master's degree or a Ph.D. who has been in jail three or four times? What do you do when a stream of potential employes casually mention they have taken their share of pinches?

The answer, much to the disappointment of youth-haters I'm sure, is that the employers probably will ignore most protest-type arrests.

Many of the protesters, burdened with throbbing social consciences, head for social work or teaching. Few cities can hire enough of them. The turnover is rapid.

Several suburban school district officials said they doubt if they'd know about the arrests in the first place, and probably wouldn't be concerned about them if they did.

Chicago's school system asks about arrests but has no flat rule against hiring someone with a record.

Even some police departments don't rule out hiring someone who has been arrested, but it is unlikely that many of today's young protesters aspire to police careers.

Several personnel directors at large companies said the question hasn't come up because they haven't had applications from people with protest arrests.

"Off hand, I'd say we wouldn't worry about a protest arrest if we needed what he could do," one personnel director said.

Another said: "So far, none of them has asked for a job, but when they do we'll probably have to decide on a policy. I imagine our policy will be rather tolerant."

Then he added: "I mean, they do plan on working some day, don't they?"

That is still another question.

MR. GROBNIK'S MONSTER HERO

If the idea of modern living theater is to involve the audience, Boris Karloff was years ahead of his time.

When he came on screen, with those electrodes jutting out of his neck, everybody in the audience did something.

There were those who suddenly remembered they had to visit the washroom. Others, more honest, simply rolled over in the seat and crouched so that their back pockets pointed at the screen.

As the suspense built, some kids slowly slid down the seat. At the moment of horror, they were out of sight on the floor.

But the most remarkable and significant reaction was that of Slats Grobnik's father.

26

Mr. Grobnik was not much of a movie fan. He always said that after a hard day in the factory, the ditch or wherever he was working, he didn't want to spend his free time watching a toothy gigolo drink champagne.

He had no screen idols. Valentino was a greaseball; Tarzan a beach bum, and Fairbanks a skinny jockey. He even thought Wallace Beery was a pretty boy.

When the original Frankenstein movie came to the neighborhood, Mr. Grobnik went only because someone told him it was about a monster in the Old Country, and he thought he might spot one of his uncles.

He wasn't impressed with the opening scenes, in which the scientist sewed the stolen body parts together and hoisted the finished monster to the roof for a jolt of lightning. Mr. Grobnik shrugged and whispered to Mrs. Grobnik: "See? Doctors. They're all the same."

Then the monster came to life and went on his antisocial binge, and a change came over Mr. Grobnik.

He identified with the monster.

It is natural for people to identify with a strong character in a movie. Usually, though, it is the hero.

But something in Boris Karloff touched a responsive chord in Mr. Grobnik.

Maybe it was that Karloff settled disputes by tossing people in the air. Maybe it was that nobody understood him, so he cracked their heads. Maybe it was that most of the hostile townspeople looked like Mr. Grobnik's relatives. Or maybe it was that the monster wasn't a pretty boy.

Whatever the reason, for the first time, somebody in a Frankenstein audience not only wasn't afraid of the monster, he was cheering for him.

When Karloff chased somebody, Mr. Grobnik bellowed encouragement. When Karloff was chained in jail, Mr. Grobnik gnashed his teeth. And when Karloff busted out Mr. Grobnik laughed triumphantly.

Even in the Biltmore theater, where audiences weren't restrained, Mr. Grobnik's reaction was offbeat. But nobody wanted to argue with somebody who sided with a monster.

Then came the final scene, in which the monster is trapped on a burning mill. As the flames engulf him, he beats on the railing with his fists in agony and anger at his tormentors below.

A strange sound was heard in the theater. Loud sobs. Mr. Grobnik sat there, holding a handkerchief against his face. He was inconsolable and was still weeping when Mrs. Grobnik led him from the theater. He had never before cried at a movie. Or even a funeral.

It always made me wonder if Hollywood really understood what they had.

The films gave today's generation a hero in Dustin Hoffman, and the 50s generation a hero in James Dean.

Hollywood maybe had the hero of Mr. Grobnik's generation and didn't know it.

Anyway, after that experience, Mr. Grobnik said he'd never go to a movie again unless it had a happy ending. He really enjoyed "Moby Dick."

SLATS' MISERY: BACK TO SCHOOL

There are times of misery in the life of any kid. Taking a bath, getting a shot, going to the dentist, getting a haircut.

But there is nothing worse than knowing that it is the last week of summer vacation, that the long, lazy days without end are somehow ending.

Even with the joyous possibility of a teacher strike that could delay the schools' opening, the kids know it is almost over.

To appreciate how deeply they suffer, just casually remind any youth between 6 and 12, or even older, that school starts next week, and isn't he happy? Then listen to the moan and whine; look at the downturned mouth; see him fling himself about in a display of grief.

That's why kids are confused when our political leaders go on TV and say a strike would be a disaster. What is so disastrous, they wonder, about a few extra days of sleeping late and bike riding. It's that kind of foolish talk that breeds distrust of politicians in the young.

If Slats Grobnik were a kid today, he'd be writing letters to the mayor urging him not to give an inch to union bullies; and then he'd write to the teachers, urging them to not be finks.

Nobody dreaded going back to school more than Slats. He couldn't stand being cooped up all day. His wild free spirit was meant to roam the wide-open alleys, 'neath the smoke-filled sky, the hot pavement under his feet. Also, he did not believe in getting up before noon. Even as a boy the sight of people going to work in the morning depressed him. "That is no way to start a day," he always said.

But in late August, Slats would suddenly change. It was as if he knew the end was near and he wanted to cram as much living into each day as it would hold.

He even looked different. His normally sleepy eyes would take on an unhealthy gleam. His slack jaw would tighten. His shuffling walk became brisk. His pallor would change to a tan. He looked terrible.

Staggering out of bed before noon, he'd be on the go all day. One minute he'd be collecting old bottles for their deposit. Then he'd be seen hitching a ride on a streetcar, or stealing a comic book from the candy store. After a round of piggy move up, he'd be ready to pitch pennies until dark. Then to the roof of a garage to drop bricks on rats.

It would be like that until the last day of freedom. Then, knowing that time had run out, he'd sit in the alley all day, brooding and thumbing through his comic books but not really seeing the pictures. In the evening, he'd go stand outside the open door of the tavern, sniffing the fumes until he had enough courage to stagger over to the schoolyard and throw a stone through one more window.

On the first morning of school, he'd be seized by the desperation and panic of a drowning man, or of a judge being asked to show his bankbook.

Lying in bed and moaning, he'd tell Mrs. Grobnik that he had everything from a stomach ache to leprosy; from a sore throat to plague.

Once he sat up half the night gulping quart after quart of water. In the morning he pointed to his bloated belly as proof his appendix was about to burst.

Another time he blew his nose so hard that it bled, and he gasped that he was dying of convulsions.

When that didn't work, he went in the parlor, slammed his fist against the wall and staggered into the kitchen with his eyes crossed, howling that he had bumped his head and couldn't see.

None of it did any good. Only once did Slats avoid the opening of school, and he did it by simply pretending to leave, then crawling under his bed and staying there all morning.

He would have made it through the afternoon, too, if he hadn't dozed off and mumbled in his sleep, giving his mother the worst fright she had since he was born. She was so relieved that it was Slats, and not a fiend, that she didn't even give him a beating. Of course, by then he was a senior in high school, so it wouldn't have mattered.

SPIRIT OF LOVE SLUGS SLATS

Some sex researchers say they have found that rock music leads to the downfall of many young ladies.

The provocative lyrics and pervasive rhythms make some girls forget the warnings their mothers gave them.

If this is true, it is another example of the push-button ease to which today's youth have become accustomed.

Young men have always sought ways to make young ladies abandon virtue. Past generations have stood beneath balconies reciting poetry. Others penned passionate letters, or learned a slinky tango.

But it was never simply a matter of popping a cassette into a stereo tape player. It took thought and initiative.

Someone like Slats Grobnik used to spend all week thinking about it. He didn't have many dates, and he knew that regardless of what happened, the girl probably wouldn't go out with him a second time, so he planned his tactics with great care.

For a while, he tried music. But this was before rock and roll. No matter how many nickels Slats put in the jukebox and played the "Hotcha Polka," "Bell-Bottom Trousers," and "Don't Fence Me In," the girl resisted.

He tried passionate love letters. But he didn't write well, so several of the girls turned the letters over to the authorities, and Slats was questioned in a couple of unsolved sex crimes.

That is when he tried poetry. Late one night he stood in a gangway next to the home of a girl, reciting a poem. But he mumbled so softly that nobody heard him, and he was picked up on suspicion of being a Peeping Tom.

Another time he tried a love potion, which he obtained from his Aunt Wanda Grobnik, who was also famous for her mystical readings and the things she could see in coffee grounds.

She gave Slats some black powder and told Slats that if he put it in a girl's food or drink, the girl would fling herself at him.

On his next date, Slats furtively sprinkled it on the girl's bowl of chili. She was sick for three days, and the Greek who owned the diner was closed down by the health department.

When nothing worked, it was inevitable that Slats would resort to the standard approach of his generation. He tried to get the girls to drink too much.

Somebody told Slats that it would work better if he took the girl some place more romantic than a tavern. So on his next date they went to the lounge at the bowling alley.

In the first hour, Slats excitedly ordered eight rounds of drinks. At exactly 9 o'clock, he toppled out of the booth and did not recover consciousness until the next morning.

Then somebody told him he should be sure to eat something heavy, so the drinks would not affect him as quickly. Before the next date he ate two plates of dumplings with gravy. He was fine until 10 o'clock, when he got sick, and the bartender threw him out.

Then somebody advised him that he should signal to a bartender to make the girl's drinks strong and his weak. On the next date, he winked at the bartender every time he ordered another round. The bartender finally punched him in the mouth.

Slats didn't quit trying, though, until a doctor told him that if he didn't stop being so romantic, he would get cirrhosis of the liver and the DTs.

He took the advice, and never again tried to use liquor to change a woman's mind about anything. At least not until he was married and the woman was his wife, and that didn't work out because he hit her with the bottle.

WHEN SLATS CAUGHT SANTA

December 26, 1969

Those of us who grew up in a big city can sometimes feel we missed out on the typical American Christmas.

The schoolbooks always showed it in a setting where people got syrup from maple trees, took sleigh rides, cut their own Christmas tree in the forest and cooked in big farm kitchens.

Yet, you never read the reminiscences of somebody like my friend Slats Grobnik. The scene of his childhood—

a second-floor flat above a tavern with the L tracks in back—is never shown on postcards.

But Slats has warm memories.

The Grobniks never cut down their own Christmas tree. They got theirs from Leo the mover, who sold trees in an empty lot next to his moving store.

Buying a tree from Leo took more skill, really, than chopping one down in the forest, because Leo was an early pioneer in creating artificial trees. But you never knew when you got one.

Leo used to spend half of his time in his garage, drilling holes in the trunks of scrawny trees, and gluing branches in to fill out the bare spots.

He'd hold up a tree, away from the glow of the street light, and say:

"Look'dis beauty. The trunk's straight as broomstick."

"It ought to be," Mr. Grobnik would say, "since the trunk happens to be a broomstick, you no-good thief."

The Grobniks never went for a sleigh ride, although Mr. Grobnik rode in a few paddy wagons, but they had a family tradition that was something like a sleigh ride.

Every Christmas eve in the middle of the afternoon, Mrs. Grobnik would bundle up Slats and his brother Fats, and they would ride a streetcar to the plant where Mr. Grobnik worked.

When he came out they would greet him and the whole family would ride home together on the streetcar.

It was partly sentiment, but it was mostly a way of making sure Mr. Grobnik didn't stop and blow his Christmas check on Division St.

In the evening, Slats and his brother would hang their stockings. The first year Slats was old enough to do this, he looked at the oil stove in the parlor and said:

"I heard on the radio where you are supposed to hang

your stocking by the fireplace. How come we ain't got a fireplace, pa?''

Slats' father explained that if they had a fireplace, and if somebody as fat as Santa could come down through it, any two-bit burglar in the neighborhood could do the same, and that's why they didn't have one.

"How's he going to get in then?" Slats asked.

"We'll leave the kitchen door unlatched," said Mrs. Grobnik, "like we do when your father goes on Division St."

Slats pointed out that Bruno, their red-eyed, black-tongued dog, would probably bite Santa, because Bruno liked to bite everybody, even the Grobniks.

Mr. Grobnik sat Slats on his knee and told how reindeer would hold Bruno at bay until Santa got the stockings stuffed. "Reindeers got horns sharp as razors," Mr. Grobnik said, "and Bruno's no fool."

Satisfied, Slats and his brother Fats would hang their stockings by the oven on the kitchen stove, the closest thing they had to a fireplace, and got into bed.

Actually, Slats used one of his father's size 16 work stockings. He later explained. "I figured a guy who had to make that many stops in one night wouldn't have time to measure nobody's feet."

And in the morning, the stockings would be loaded to the brim, and by the time they sat down to Christmas dinner, so was Mr. Grobnik.

Like all kids, Slats had to find out one day that there was no Santa. He still remembers.

He was awakened during the night by the sound of somebody moving about in the kitchen.

Slats crept from his bed, hoping at last to catch a glimpse of Santa.

But there, by the kitchen stove, stood his father in his long underwear, his arms loaded with gifts.

Slats bounded through the kitchen into his parents' bedroom, howling:

"Ma, get up quick—pa's filching every damn present Santa left for us!"

So that's when his parents decided—when Slats picked up the phone and started yelling for the cops—that he ought to know the truth.

THE
GROBNIK
"SURVIVAL
KIT"

As an annual service to partygoers, here are some New Year's Eve social tips from that well known social arbiter, Slats Grobnik.

They are taken from his best-selling book, "My 30 New Year's Eves Without an Arrest."

What to Wear: The current "in" garments are Edwardian suits for men and maxicoats and dresses for women, or the reverse if you really want to whoop it up. White turtlenecks and bowling-league shirts are no longer très chic. Regardless of what you wear, the most important consideration is that it can be thrown in the furnace and burned the next day.

What to Drink: Select one favorite beverage and stay with it all evening, and all the next day if you wish. I recommend the always-festive Boilermaker. (Recipe: Pour one shot of whisky down your throat. Follow with one glass of beer.) After midnight, the ingredients can be mixed in a glass, vase or pot.

At midnight, the traditional drink is champagne. But remember, never drink it straight from the bottle unless the hostess does so first.

I don't recommend the popular practice of drinking from whatever glass happens to be near your arm. But those who enjoy doing so should remember to check the glass for cigaret butts.

Dining Hints: Many hostesses plan a post-midnight buffet. If you are a guest at such a party, keep a few hints in mind: Before putting the food on your lap, remember to sit down. And be sure that the food is on a plate. Cold chicken, pizza, sandwiches and pickles can be eaten with the fingers. But do not use your fingers while eating Jello-mold salad or ice cream.

Miscellaneous Hints: If you feel a bit groggy, and think you might be lapsing into unconsciousness, try to find a bedroom. But do not select a bed in which the host's children are sleeping. If you choose a bed that is covered with hats and coats, remember to remove your shoes. If you feel a need to rest on the bathroom floor, or in the tub itself, be courteous and do not lock the door behind you.

Sometime during the evening, you may need a breath of fresh air. Don't lean out a window, especially if it is higher than the basement. A short walk is the best idea. But remember to wear a coat and shoes, and write down the host's address and pin it to your lapel. Try not to lie down in a snowbank, a doorway or on the sidewalk, as this can bring on frostbite and gangrene, which just makes the day-after blues more uncomfortable.

The big moment at any New Year's Eve party is midnight (although some purists argue that the big moment is the first fight or the first crying jag). Try to pace yourself so you are still conscious at midnight, or arrange to have somebody gently slap you awake.

It is customary and perfectly proper for the men to kiss the ladies. Other variations of course, depend on local custom. It is considered bad form for a man to kiss a woman more than three times, without her consent. (And unless her husband has passed out.) In any case, all kissing should end no later than noon the next day.

When to Leave: The host and hostess usually give a gentle hint. Watch them, and when the host's head falls back and his eyes roll upwards, and his breathing comes in gasps, and the hostess is quietly sobbing as she studies her furniture, rug and coffee table, it is a good time to slip away. It is always a nice gesture for a guest to send a little note the following week, offering to pay for any windows smashed in the festivities.

A Final Tip for the Hostess: The next day, look under the cushions of the sofa for lost jewelry, under the bed for scarves, hats and gloves and, of course, under the basement steps and behind the furnace for lingering guests.

MRS. GROBNIK A CHECK-UPPER

A Chicago bank has hired a creature named Gucci to design arty new checks and checkbooks.

Gucci, who is famous for designing women's shoes and purses, has created checks with swans, daisies, mist-shrouded trees, rippling water, a sunrise and even a seagull against a lavender background. Gucci is not the hairy-chested type.

The bank thinks this will attract new customers. Maybe it will, but I won't be one of them.

Banks should be serious. My attitude toward them is the same as that of Mrs. Grobnik, who was Slats Grobnik's mother. "A good bank," she always said, "should look like a jail, except the bank's walls should be thicker."

Whenever she made a deposit—and she never made withdrawals—Mrs. Grobnik would walk around the lobby to see if they had hired any new guards. If she found one, she would ask him:

"Are you a good shot?"

They always said yes, so she'd ask:

"Who have you shot?"

If they hadn't shot anybody, she would go to the chief cashier and ask why they were hiring inexperienced people.

Sometimes she would purposely include a half-dollar in her deposit. If the cashier didn't bite it, she would triumphantly report him to the vice president.

Once in a while, she would set the alarm clock for 1 a.m. Then she'd get up and walk to the bank and rap on the door. When the night guard peered out, she'd say: "Remember, no sleeping."

After using the same bank for 24 years, she abruptly closed her account and put her money somewhere else. The reason was that a cashier had grown a mustache.

"The next thing," she said, "is he will take my money and run away to Las Vegas."

I'm sure that Mrs. Grobnik would not have felt comfortable with Gucci's checkbooks. In fact, she never in her life used a checkbook. She thought that anybody who would put their money in a bank, then immediately spend a nickel writing a check to get some of it out, should be put away by his relatives for his own good.

Mrs. Grobnik finally stopped dealing with banks entirely when she found out that they loaned money. She had always thought they just stored it away. It was her opinion that anybody who borrowed money did so because they didn't have enough of their own, which means they were bums. And she didn't want to trust her money to an institution that would loan it out to bums.

I'm not quite as conservative as Mrs. Grobnik about

such matters, but the business of the Gucci checks would make me nervous.

For one thing, his name isn't just plain Gucci. No Italian mother is going to send a boy into the world with no more of a handle than "Gucci." Would an Italian priest baptize a baby as plain "Gucci"?

Yet, when I called the bank and asked them what Gucci's full name was, they said they didn't know.

Maybe being just Gucci is enough for the fashion circles in New York, but a bank ought to get a guy's first name before they do any kind of business with him. If they hire somebody who goes around saying "I am Gucci," they might decide to lend money to people who walk in and say, "I am Smith—give me a thou."

I am not opposed to adding a little art to checks. But it should be something serious. When a person writes a check he shouldn't think about daisies, seagulls, rippling waters, sunrises, trees and other pleasant things. He is spending money, and he should think dark thoughts.

If there are going to be daisies on the check, they should be surrounding a gravestone with his name on it. If there are going to be rippling waters, a hand should be sticking out of the water. If there is a tree, it should have a noosed rope attached to a limb.

I'd like to see checkbooks with pictures of a turnip, with a drop or two of blood oozing out of it.

Many men would like checks for their wives that would bear a drawing of a widow in black, sitting at a lawyer's desk, with the lawyer saying: "Well, you can always sell the furniture."

Or maybe a bleak, rickety old building with a sign over the door that says: "Poor House."

Married men could use personalized checks with a snappy slogan across the top. Maybe something like: "Bartender: Please don't cash this. Signed, His children."

HAS PINOCHLE LOST ITS WHACK?

October 14, 1970

This is nothing against Vincent L. Bonus. He won his title fair and square and I don't begrudge it to him. But it doesn't seem right.

Vincent Bonus is now the city's official pinochle champion. He beat out more than 300 other players a few nights ago in the Park District's tournament, so he must be good.

But he just doesn't look or sound like a great pinochle player.

For one thing, he doesn't have an accent. I don't remember any great players who didn't have one. And if not a foreign accent, at least a West Side accent.

45

In fact, he is a college-educated mathematics whiz who has an executive job at a steel company and a house in the suburbs. His mathematical mind is what makes him good, he says.

And where did he learn pinochle? At a kitchen table from uncles? In a neighborhood tavern? At least in a firehouse?

Vincent Bonus said he learned to play pinochle from a girl at college.

"We used to play pinochle all the time," he said. And he didn't even look embarrassed about admitting such a thing.

As good as he may be, Vincent L. Bonus being a pinochle champion is like Charles Percy being a pool hustler.

In fact, I'm suspicious of the entire Park District tournament. Not only because it is run by the city, which is enough in itself to make me want to put all the cards under infra-red lights, but because of the way the players acted.

They sat there, all 300 of them, dropping the cards gently or sliding them to the middle of the table.

Nowhere in the entire tournament was there a single knuckle-whacker. Not one player smashed his cards to the table with a fist-jarring blow. And this, as scholars of the game can tell you, has always been the mark of a superior player.

When they played, the game had a sound all its own. It was, whack, whack, whack, with an occasional grunt of joy, a pop of a beer cap, and between hands a bit of constructive criticism, such as: "You're a real jackass, you know dat?"

That's why pinochle has traditionally been played on kitchen tables, bars or booths. The modern home card table would be shattered after one hand was played.

Possibly the most powerful card delivery I have ever seen belonged to Slats Grobnik's father, Mr. Grobnik.

His backswing was deceptively slow. He would raise the card in a motion similar to a man reaching up to tip his hat. Then, shifting his weight to his belly, which would be pressed against the table, his right hand would come flashing down with the speed and force of a nightstick approaching a Yippie's head.

Once, it had almost tragic results. Slats happened to lean across the table to get a hard-boiled egg just as Mr. Grobnik was playing a card, and the blow caught Slats full on the brow. He was out for 15 minutes and for several days he couldn't see straight.

Mr. Grobnik's right-hand knuckles became so famous that when the WPA put in a new sidewalk, the precinct captain had him put his knuckle-prints in the wet cement. He was the only player so honored.

Another strange thing about the Park District tournament was that the players were polite. "Everyone has a nice time," Mr. Bonus said, as he received congratulations for his victory.

That is like Dick Butkus playing chucking a quarterback under the chin.

The proper competitive spirit in pinochle was epitomized by a man I read about who was in a game in a Gary tavern one hot night.

His partner made a serious mistake, so he leaped up, shouted, "You should have led me in trump," and shot him.

Mr. Bonus also said he felt little tension during his victory. "I was quite relaxed," he said.

I remember reading about a night watchman who drew a one-in-a-million hand—all eight aces. He stood up, smiled and fell over dead.

I would be dishonest if I claimed to have been a genuine knuckle-whacking pinochle player myself. It isn't easy to admit, but I wasn't.

Oh, for years I tried all right. And I played with some real knuckle-whackers. But they finally barred me. As Mr. Grobnik put it:

"You better give up. We'll all be disgraced if somebody listens and keeps hearing 'whack-whack-whack-owweeeee!' "

A
CRACKING
GOOD
TALENT

August 9, 1971

The first time Slats Grobnik cracked one of his knuckles, dogs all over the neighborhood began barking, and a squad car came by to see who had been shot. Slats knew then that he had a special gift.

He could get two resounding cracks out of each finger—one from the knuckle and one from the middle joint. And he could get one out of each of his thumbs. That made 18 of them, and when he did it fast, it was like a string of Zebra fire-crackers.

It worried his mother for a while. She thought there might be something wrong with him, so she took him to the doctor who had an office upstairs over the drugstore to have him examined. The doctor told her that Slats had real loud knuckles and charged her $10. As they walked home Slats said: "I would have told you that for a quarter."

The sound bothered some people. In school he cracked them during tests because he liked to see the teacher jump. She finally made him wear heavy, fleece-lined gloves to muffle the sound. It was more peaceful, but by the time everybody else was reading at the seventh-grade level, Slats was still trying to get his first book opened.

He liked cracking his knuckles in the movies best, especially during the romantic scenes. When Charles Boyer was kissing Bette Davis, Slats would clasp his hands together and race through all 18 knuckles. The audience thought that Bette Davis' teeth were breaking. Who knows what they would think during the romantic scenes in today's movies.

As he got older, his knuckles grew even louder. Every summer, Slats was given the job as starter at the alderman's neighborhood olympics. For a while, the alderman had used a regular starter who fired a blank pistol, but instead of running the race, most of the neighborhood youths put their hands in the air or emptied their pockets. So they let Slats crack his big knuckle, which was louder anyway.

During the winter, when the softball season was over, Slats was sponsored by Crazy Al's Tavern to crack his knuckles in competition with representatives of other taverns.

He lost only one match out of hundreds. And that loss, surprisingly, was to Mrs. Ruby Peak, an elderly widow who lived above the war surplus store and represented Bruno's Tap. Mrs. Peak had a left knee that cracked like a rifle shot. It took her almost four hours of steady cracking to beat Slats that one time, but after that Mrs. Peak walked funny.

People who couldn't crack their knuckles loud, or at all, were always asking Slats how he did it.

Like most great natural athletes he was modest about

his talent. He'd say things like: "I guess somebody up there likes to hear my knuckles pop." Or: "I could never have done it without my mother and father who both got big hands."

He once appeared on the Morris B. Sachs Radio Amateur Hour, cracking his knuckles in time to "Lady of Spain I Adore You." He did well, too, finishing in the judging behind a boy who clicked his teeth to "Lady of Spain I Adore You" and a girl who toe-danced while playing "Lady of Spain I Adore You" on her accordion.

Somebody once asked Slats why his knuckles, or anybody else's knuckles for that matter, made a cracking noise. Slats who could be philosophical, said: "What else are they good for?"

His answer satisfied him, and it satisfied me. Some things should not be explored too deeply or the mystery is destroyed. Look what has happened to sex.

But now scientists, who can't leave anything alone, claim to have found the reason for the cracking sound that knuckles make.

Some British researchers did it by using special knuckle-cracking machines, X-rays and other measuring devices on a team of volunteers.

They have found this answer: There is fluid in the knuckle joints. When people stretch these joints, tiny gas bubbles form in the fluid. When you bend your fingers forward, the gas makes a popping noise. Then the gas goes back into the fluid and if you wait awhile, you can repeat the process.

Big deal. Now that they have figured that out, they'll probably start working on the question of why some people can wiggle their ears and others can't.

Slats could really wiggle his. For a while, he even thought he had solved the mystery of flight. But that's another story.

GROBNIK
FIELD
CHOSEN
AS
SITE!

The site for the First Annual Chicago-Area Open Penny Pitching Championship Tournament has been selected.

It will not cost the taxpayers a nickel and it won't use up any of the lakefront.

The tournament will be held Sunday, Aug. 15, in a parking lot a few steps north of this newspaper plant, 401 N. Wabash. Starting time is 1 p.m.

Purists will exclaim: "What? Lagging pennies on anything but a sidewalk is contrary to tradition."

Yes, but the purists have never tried to find a stretch of sidewalk long enough to accommodate a major tournament. If

51

enough contestants turn out for the event, the players would be strung out for a mile.

Also, the sidewalks in the downtown area, where the tournament must be held because of public transportation facilities, are the wrong size.

Thus, the parking lot as a site. Lines will be painted on the playing surface to provide 10-foot lags, the length specified for both national and international competition.

At least five taverns are within a short walk of the playing field, a factor that helped sway the site committee.

Because Wabash Av. is elevated at this location, spectators will be able to watch the matches from above, cheering their favorites and shouting obscenities at others.

Benny Bentley, the veteran sports promoter, will broadcast a lag-by-lag account of the key matches over a public address system.

Bentley, a onetime Humboldt Park-area penny lagging champion, provided a few tips for those who will be competing for the first time:

"You got to loosen up before you start lagging. The best way to do this is to wiggle your thumb three or four times and snap your fingers once or twice. But not too much, or you'll be tired before you start.

"It's a good idea to avoid letting cold drafts on your thumb, too. Never sleep with your thumb by an open window because it'll stiffen up on you, or something might bite it."

I asked Bentley if great penny laggers, like natural hitters and boxers, are "born" or if they can be developed.

"Anybody can become a great lagger," he said. "You give me a kid and if he has the basic physical ability—which includes laziness, shiftlessness, cunning, and greed—I'll make a champion of him.

"The main thing is dedication. You can't get to be a great penny lagger if you spend your time hanging around libraries and church basements. You got to be willing to put in hour after hour on a street corner."

Bentley will also act as chief referee. As such, he will settle disputes over the rules. He will carry the traditional leather-covered sap and a can of Mace.

Other referees will include Sam Sianis, a tavern keeper, and Jon Anderson, a columnist. William Singer and Leon Despres, both of whom are aldermen, have also agreed to act as referees and to submit to a search before they leave the premises.

THE RULES WILL BE SIMPLE:

All players must provide their own penny.

Each match will be played to 10 points. Side bets will not be tolerated, unless you can get away with it. Injuries suffered by anybody who welshes on a side bet are his own responsibility.

No spitting on the playing surface or your opponent.

The referee's word is final. Anybody punching a referee loses one point.

Contestants must give their names to one of the referees when they arrive. They will be paired with a preliminary opponent. Winners of the preliminaries will go on to the next round of matches. This will continue until a champion has been crowned.

The grand champion will receive the Grobnik Trophy, the symbol of penny pitching supremacy.

The runner-up will receive the Willie Hyena Trophy.

Semi-finalists will be awarded some kind of do-dads.

The parking lot—which will be known as Grobnik Stadium for this event—is easy to reach by public transportation, car, bicycle or on foot.

It's a couple of blocks north of the Loop. The north-south subway's Grand Av. station is nearby.

This contest is open to everybody, male or female, of any age, from city or suburb. Only disk jockeys are barred. We have to have some standards.

THE
DAY
SLATS
FELL
FOR
A
GIRL

Valentine's Day was never one of Slats Grobnik's favorite events. He was just a toddler when he saw a card with a drawing of a heart, pierced by an arrow, but his reaction was: "Good shot."

He preferred Halloween, when he could spring from dark gangways or drop from a tree and unnerve pedestrians. He did this the rest of the year, too, but on Halloween fewer people complained to his parents.

Valentine's Day meant nothing to Slats because he didn't think much of girls. As he put it: "When you hit 'em, they cry. They must be queer."

Year after year, he was the only kid in school who didn't bring valentine cards to class. He brought envelopes, but they contained notes saying things like: "This is your final warning. Give me a nickel or I'll bend your bicycle spokes."

Naturally, he was the only boy who didn't receive any valentines. Once, a teacher mistakenly felt sorry for him and gave him a card. He promptly reported her to the principal, saying: "Next, she'll be molesting me."

His mother used to tease him about his indifference to girls. She said: "Why do you think your father comes home at night?"

Slats thought about that, and said: "Because the tavern closes?"

Later, his mother worried about his attitude, so she consulted his Aunt Wanda Grobnik, who was famous for her seances and readings of coffee grounds. Aunt Wanda looked at Slats' palms for a long time. Then she carefully felt his skull. And she concluded: "He's dirty. Maybe a bath would help."

His father tried talking to him. He thought Slats might appreciate girls if he explained the facts of life.

Slats listened carefully. Then he went to his mother and said: "Get yourself a gun, Ma. If he tries that stuff, no jury in the world would convict you."

But it finally happened. A new girl moved into the neighborhood. On her first day at school, Slats punched her on the arm, as he did with all newcomers. He waited for her to cry. Instead, she threw a rock at his head.

Slats found her irresistible. He had never met a girl like her before, and the change in him was remarkable.

He began washing his neck every day, his ears every second day. He changed stockings every morning, switching them with his brother, Fats Grobnik.

He even poured great quantities of Brilliantine on his hair, although he still wouldn't comb it.

The girl wasn't impressed. So Slats tried to dazzle her with some of the athletic feats that had made him famous.

"Watch," he said, and with a loud hissing sound, he would spit through his teeth halfway across the street, a neighborhood record.

But she still threw rocks at his head.

So he tried a different approach. He stared at her, the way he had seen Charles Boyer stare at a woman in a movie. With one eyelid drooping.

He would sit in school staring that way for hours. The girl didn't notice. But the teacher did, and she gave him better grades because, in the past, both eyelids had drooped.

The staring routine finally caused trouble when the girl noticed him and screamed. But that's because it was almost midnight, and he was sitting in a tree outside her window.

This was when he worked up enough courage to actually talk to her. He decided to do it by phone. But when he called her, and she answered, he was so confused that he just stood there, breathing heavily into the phone.

He was still standing there, breathing heavily into the phone, when the police traced the call and got to the phone booth. They let him go after he promised not to do it again. "It already cost me one nickel," he said. "I'm no playboy."

In desperation, he decided to give her a handmade valentine. When the day came, he asked his mother what it should say, and she suggested he write something romantic.

He nodded and began writing. It came to almost six pages. He put it in an envelope, went to school, and left it on the girl's desk.

The girl read it, then showed it to the teacher, who took it to the principal, who called in a juvenile officer.

"That's the way my father explained it to me," Slats said, so they let him go.

It was the last time Slats tried being romantic. From then on, he threw rocks at the girl's head, and stopped changing his stockings. His Aunt Wanda nodded and predicted that he would marry young.

EASTER BUNNY LAYS AN EGG

March 31, 1972

Some kids lose their illusions sooner than others. And when it came to the Easter Bunny and Santa Claus, nobody lost them any earlier than Slats Grobnik.

He was just a mere child, so young he hadn't started smoking, when he told his mother he doubted that an Easter bunny went around leaving candy-filled baskets for children. He said:

"No rabbit would come in this neighborhood. He'd be run over by a beer truck."

It wasn't that his childish imagination couldn't create fantasies. He believed in many creatures he had never seen. He believed in the Peeping Tom, the second-story man and old creeps who hid behind bushes.

But he rejected Santa and the Bunny for a simple and

logical reason. As he argued: "Anybody who can get in and out of that many houses without being seen is going to take stuff, not leave it."

When he began school a kindergarten teacher asked the class to tell her who came tiptoeing into their homes on Christmas morning, when everyone was sound asleep. The class chorused "Santa!" Slats shouted: "My fodder, and my mudder yells at him."

When the teacher asked who came down the chimney, Slats said: "Anybody comes down our chimney is nuts. He'd end up in the oil stove in the kitchen."

The teacher suggested that he might come through a window. Slats said: "Our dog would take his foot off. He even bites my fodder."

Yet, Slats left open the possibility that he could be wrong, and if so, he didn't want to miss a chance for something free.

So when Easter came, he was ready. After everybody was asleep, he got a ball of string and set traps all over the flat. He figured that if the Easter Bunny really existed, he could capture it and demand an extra basket in exchange for freedom.

At dawn, Mr. Grobnik quietly got up and brought Slats' basket out of a closet, to put it in the parlor. But he tripped over the string and cracked his head on the ice box.

The sight of his father sitting on the floor dazed, with the basket in his hand, was the evidence Slats needed that the Easter Bunny did, indeed, exist.

He cried joyously: "Look, ma, the bunny really left me a basket. And pa was stealing it. Call the cops."

His new belief carried over to the next morning when the neighborhood's annual Easter egg hunt, sponsored by the precinct captain, was held in the vacant lot next to Bruno's Tavern.

When his mother explained that the Easter rabbit had

hidden chocolate eggs and other treats all over the vacant lot, Slats said: "That's an all-right rabbit. I hope no drunk hunter ever shoots him."

But Slats grew suspicious when a couple of other kids were finding most of the eggs. And one of them, Skinny Archie, was usually so dumb he couldn't find his teeth with his tongue.

Afterwards, Slats got Archie alone and questioned him closely while sitting on his chest. Archie confessed that he and the other kid were so lucky because their fathers always displayed the biggest pictures of the aldermen in their windows at election time. So the night before, the precinct captain had shown them a map of the eggs.

That's when Slats finally realized the Bunny didn't exist, but that clout and the fix did. He was so mad he went to the precinct captain and threatened to tell everyone unless he got to see the map next year, which he did.

But after that experience, Easter didn't mean much to Slats. All the other kids would wash their necks and feet and put on their best shirts, ties and jackets. Not Slats. He would wear his Halloween costume, which made him look like a very large bat. He liked to drop out of a tree and startle the old ladies of the neighborhood, as they returned from church after having their food-filled Easter baskets blessed.

A few years later, everyone was surprised to see Slats himself show up at the church, carrying a basket of sausage, eggs and other traditional foods. He was even well dressed, in a purple zoot suit.

Seeing him having a basket blessed convinced everybody that he had mended his ways and would go on to great things; maybe even a steady job.

But they didn't see him when he arrived home. He reached under the food and withdrew a deck of cards and a pair of dice, saying: "You never know what'll give you the edge."

HOW
SLATS
LOST
HIS
MARBLES

Since the warm weather arrived, I haven't seen even one kid playing marbles. It looks like the game is dead.

But what killed it? The sociologists haven't explained, so we can only guess.

Maybe it is because today's youths are so rich. They have seized the nation's economy and can buy what they want. A bag of marbles isn't an impressive possession. The only people poor enough to appreciate a bag of marbles are the parents, but they are too busy working for their children to have time for marbles.

Maybe it is because nobody plays marbles on TV.

Most of the games youngsters play have been popularized on TV. Golf, bowling, and sex, for example.

Frankly, I don't feel any sense of loss at the decline of marbles. I played it a lot, but I wasn't very good. But, then, nobody in the neighborhood was in the same class as Slats Grobnik.

Many great athletes are born with special physical gifts that make them "naturals."

Wilt Chamberlain, with his height, was a born basketball player, and Teddy Williams, with his remarkable eyesight, was a natural hitter.

With Slats, it was his thumb.

He was blessed with an extraordinarily long, double-jointed thumb. Nobody had a thumb as long as Slats'. Nobody had fingers as long as Slats' thumb.

And it was powerful. He was constantly exercising it, sitting for hours every night and just flicking it. His thumb muscles got bigger than his biceps. The girls at the North Av. beach laughed at his strange physique, but he didn't care. He'd pick up a rock and flick it out beyond the breakwaters.

When he'd kneel, dig his knuckles in the dirt, and unleash his shot, his thumb made a whooshing sound like that of a golf swing.

Slats also had the self-confidence of a natural athlete. When he heard the story of David and Goliath, Slats shrugged and said: "I could of done the same thing with a marble."

He became so well known that his alderman heard about him and got excited. There used to be a big-city marble championship and the alderman figured that if someone from his ward won, he'd get his picture in the paper for something besides a malfeasance indictment.

The alderman went to Slats' house and promised his parents that if Slats won he would have a city job some day.

Slats cried hysterically until his mother explained that he wouldn't really have to work.

After that, Slats did nothing but practice and polish his supershooter.

He thought his shooter had mysterious powers of its own, because it had been given to him by his late Aunt Wanda, who was well known for her spiritual consultations and fortunes. Slats even called the shooter "Aunt Wanda" and believed he could not lose with it, or win without it.

On the morning of the tournament, Slats was calm. He ate a hearty breakfast of Twinkies and Pepsi.

Then it happened.

The shooter rolled off the kitchen table and fell to the floor, where his baby brother, Fats Grobnik, was crawling. Fats popped it into his mouth and swallowed it. He swallowed everything, which is why he was called Fats.

Slats was pale when he came out and announced: "Fats swallowed Aunt Wanda. I ain't playing."

The alderman showed up with a quart of mineral oil, but Mrs. Grobnik wouldn't let him in the house.

After that, Slats never again played marbles. And it was a long time before he lost his bitterness and stopped dropping shoehorns and roller-skate keys near his brother.

SLATS GROBNIK WAS NO 13-MAN

May 9, 1972

This is the dark day—Friday the 13th—when we must all beware of such unlucky happenings as our paths being crossed by an alderman.

Some people defy the bad-luck tradition. There are clubs made up of people who delight in breaking mirrors and walking under ladders. But I've never been a member of such clubs. Long ago, I learned from Slats Grobnik that there is indeed something sinister and very real in most of the superstitions.

There was nobody more superstitious than Slats. One year he pleaded with his parents, Mr. and Mrs. Grobnik, to take him and his little brother, Fats, out of town until Friday the 13th. He said:

"That's the Chicago Machine for ya'."

He tried to ward off the day's bad luck by getting good-luck charms from his Aunt Wanda Grobnik, who was famous for her ability to read tea leaves, coffee grounds, and to look into the future. Her powers as a seer were such that she could look at Slats when he was only a year old and say: "He'll grow up to be a bum." Even Slats later said she was accurate.

One year she prepared Slats for Friday the 13th by giving him dozens of different kinds of magical roots and herbs and leaves. He was showing them to the Greek who ran the ice cream parlor when a detective looked in the window and immediately pinched the Greek for being a pusher. As the Greek was being put in the paddy wagon, Slats yelled: "I told you it was a bad day."

Another time, Slats was so afraid to go outside that he went into a closet, closed the door, and sat on the floor.

He finally dozed off and began snoring. His mother didn't know he was in the closet, so when she heard the terrible sound, she ran next door to the candy store and phoned the police.

They burst in and grabbed Slats, who began kicking and howling, so one of them hit him on the head with a billy, raising such a terrible bump that for the first time Slats' head had a normal shape.

The incident prompted Slats to observe: "You can't hide from bad luck."

On another Friday the 13th, Slats tried to be a good citizen. He wanted to warn people that there were bad spirits in the air, so he stood in a dark gangway. When somebody walked by he would hiss something like: "Hey, lady, something bad could happen to you."

The third woman had him arrested.

He would become even more careful than usual about such things as not stepping on a line in a sidewalk. He walked that way all of his life, taking different-length steps to avoid the lines: a little step, a long, loping stride.

He was walking that way through a strange neighborhood one night when a woman happened to look over her shoulder, saw him approaching, and began screaming. Slats barely escaped from a neighborhood mob.

Black cats across his path terrified him more than anything else. He saw one come out of a house one day and trotted sideways to keep it from crossing his path. He trotted sideways right across Milwaukee Av., causing a motorist to swerve to avoid hitting him. Instead the motorist hit a light pole.

As the firemen loaded the driver onto a stretcher, Slats leaned over and said: "Mister, you ought to be more careful about those black cats."

When he got older, Slats' superstitions didn't diminish. They got even worse. On a Friday the 13th, he would tell his wife: "If anything happens to me, I don't want you to be involved. I'll go to the tavern."

One year, he sat in the tavern all day and all evening, worrying and drinking. The bartender would tell him not to worry, but Slats would look sly and say: "You'll see." Then he would worry and drink some more.

At exactly one minute before midnight, he fell off the stool and cracked his head. When the police hauled him away, he was muttering something about "bad spirits," so they pulled the tavern's license for spiking drinks, Slats told the bartender: "I told you you'd see."

SLATS GROBNIK, SIDEWALK MAN

May 10, 1972

The Arlington Heights police are said to have put some kind of ban on the playing of sidwalk hopscotch.

If they are serious, which I doubt, it could not be enforced. It would be a violation of an unwritten common law that says sidewalks belong to kids.

Adults may use them for walking on, plunging to, or shoveling off, but basically sidewalks are really long, narrow playgrounds.

The best place for a child to play and learn is on a sidewalk. It is his natural environment. If you take a child into the woods, he can fall out of a tree and break a leg and ruin the weekend.

Nobody liked sidewalks more than I did, except Slats Grobnik. To this day, if he walks on grass for more than five minutes, his feet blister. His attitude toward lawns and gardens is summed up when he looks sick and says: "Worms live in that stuff."

When the rest of us would go to Humboldt Park, Slats would shake his head and stay behind, saying: "Anything that can hide behind a fireplug is small enough for me to handle, but how do I know what kind of creep is in the bushes?" He feared being kidnaped and held for ransom because he knew his father didn't believe in touching the savings.

When we built a tree house, Slats wouldn't come up. He said:

"If people was meant to live in trees, the squirrels would slip some nuts to the city building inspector."

So Slats always stayed on the sidewalk and did the things all kids do. And some that nobody had heard of before.

One summer, he spent all of July pitching pennies. He got so good that one Sunday morning he made 14 straight liners. The precinct captain had that penny bronzed and it was hung up behind the bar of the corner tavern. Later, Slats' mother put it in with his bronzed baby shoes and his first tooth, a one-inch molar, incidentally.

Naturally, he sold lemonade on the sidewalk. We all did. But Slats was the only one who could sell it when the weather was cold. Even in November he'd have a dozen customers lined up.

One day a plainclothes cop happened to get in line and that's when they found out that with every glass you got to look at the dirty pictures Slats found in his father's dresser. And that was years before Hugh Hefner came along.

There were days when Slats would just draw or write

on the sidewalk with chalk or stones. Mostly dirty words. Then he'd hide in a gangway and peek out to see if ladies were offended. If they were, he'd go "hee-hee." Slats would have been a natural hippie.

Sometimes he'd spend the day just lying on the sidewalk, face down, forehead pressed against the pavement, not moving a muscle. He'd be watching the ants in the crack. People from outside the neighborhood were startled, especially when he'd hiss: "Boy, they're murdering each other."

Once a drunk came out of the tavern and tripped over him. Slats pretended to have a broken rib and the drunk gave him $5 to keep quiet. Slats moaned louder and he got $5 more. For a long time after that, Slats thought about going to law school.

Even when he didn't feel like doing anything, Slats did it on the sidewalk. He liked to lean against a wall and spit. That wasn't as disgusting as it sounds, although it was pretty disgusting.

He'd just stand there, not moving or saying anything, and every two or three minutes he'd go "phttt" between his two front teeth. He'd keep it up all day, quitting only when he felt weak from dehydration.

A big event for Slats was when a new section of sidewalk was put down.

He'd sneak out at night, take off his shoe, and put his footprint on it.

His feet are hard to describe. They were very big and shaped kind of funny.

So people got nervous when they saw the print. But a man from a museum came out and said there was nothing to worry about because whatever made the print had been dead for millions of years.

What Slats was best at was walking on a sidewalk without stepping on lines. We all did that for good luck when we happened to be walking, but Slats would go walking for hours just to avoid stepping on lines.

One day he decided to try for a world's record and he left without telling anybody. He was gone for three days, walking all over the city, avoiding stepping on lines.

When he got back home, he yelled: "Don't worry, ma, I wasn't kidnaped."

His father waved the bank book and triumphantly said: "See, I was right. There was no reason to disturb the interest."

GROBNIK'S BOUT WITH U.S. DEBT

Nobody is surprised when kids of 15 or younger are arrested at protest demonstrations, because young people are more interested in national issues than they used to be.

But that does not mean that past generations of youths were oblivious to the grave issues of their time, or that they didn't take action and get involved.

All during his boyhood my friend Slats Grobnik brooded about the national debt.

Nobody says much about it anymore, but the national debt used to be of great concern to everybody, especially Republican politicians and the Tribune. In his editorials,

71

Col. McCormick always sounded like he was going to be stuck with the whole tab, plus tip.

Every time the national debt went up, the stories would go into detail as to how much every man, woman, and child in the country owed.

The first time Slats heard that on the radio, he was just a boy, but he ran around the Grobnik flat pulling down the window shades, turned out the lights, crawled under the bed, and yelled to his mother to tell anybody who looked like a bill collector that he wasn't home and that she didn't know when he was expected back.

Because of the national debt, Slats became the best arithmetic student in our class. But then he flunked everything else. He would spend the day furiously figuring out how long it would take him to pay his share on his present income, which consisted of the two-cent deposits he received for taking bottles back to the candy store.

While everybody else would be studying history or geography, Slats would be bent over his calculations, occasionally moaning: "I'll be in the hole until I'm 90." He was only in the fifth grade when he began taking double-strength Maalox for his stomach.

Slats was ahead of his time in many ways. For instance, he didn't hesitate to rebuke the older generation for not having faced up to the problem of the national debt.

He was always startling adults on the street by hissing: "Whyn't you pay your bills, you cheapskate." One nervous man thought Slats was the bookie's son and stuffed $5 in his hand.

Slats was most bothered when the Republicans would warn that if the national debt wasn't paid, the burden would pass to the next generation.

One night at dinner he called his father a deadbeat for welshing on his share of the national debt and sticking Slats with it. Mr. Grobnik was so impressed by Slats' precocity that he struck him on the head with a soup spoon, making Slats one of the earliest victims of adult repression and establishing a generation gap in the Grobnik household, as well as an indentation in Slats' skull.

That forced Slats to use underground tactics. He took to leaving anonymous notes to his father in the mailbox. They said things like: "Your share of the national debt is $897. You know what happens to deadbeats."

And: "If you don't pay up soon, we will snatch your son Slats." That night Mr. Grobnik left the bedroom window open in Slats' room.

Slats, way back then, tried appealing to the conscience of the business establishment. He wrote letters to the tavern saying they should not give Mr. Grobnik any more credit because he was already $897 in debt to the federal government.

When that didn't work, Slats went right to the top, writing directly to the President. He said:

"Responsible for my personal debts only and not for my father's national debt.

"Don't believe him if he says he doesn't have enough money to pay. He's got lots of money in the bank on Milwaukee Av. and the bankbook can be found in the bedroom drawer under where he keeps his winter underwear. Let me know when you will send somebody over to get it and I will make sure that the dog is tied up. Take it and leave me alone."

When he didn't get a reply, he wrote: "I never bought anything from you, so how can you say I owe you money?"

Finally he wrote: "Will you settle for $2.50? If not, you can sue. Take it or leave it."

Slats didn't stop worrying until years later when somebody told him that we owed the national debt to ourselves. He felt good for a while, but he started brooding about that, too. And the last time I saw him, he was writing letters to people he knew, saying: "When are you going to pay me?"

SLATS' SEARCH FOR MUSCLES

Charles Atlas, who died a few days ago at 80, sold mail-order exercise courses to millions of men and boys who wanted a V-shaped body. One of them was Slats Grobnik.

Slats was really skinny. A lot of kids are so thin that their ribs stand out. But with Slats, if he stood in a strong light, you could see the outline of his vital organs.

Slats didn't care. In fact, he didn't want muscles. He always said: "If you have muscles, somebody might hire you to work."

And being that skinny didn't keep him from enjoying athletics because his favorite sports were penny-pitching and standing on a corner, spitting between his teeth.

But, as is often the case, it was a girl that finally changed Slats' mind about muscles. And it happened on a beach, in the classic Charles Atlas manner.

One day Slats was lying on the North Av. Beach and a pretty girl ran by and kicked sand in his face.

Slats jumped up and threw sand in her face.

So she punched him in the jaw and knocked him down. Then she kicked more sand on him and walked away.

As he slunk from the beach, he vowed to build up his body and return to the beach and give her the beating she deserved.

At first he wasn't sure how to go about it, so he asked his father, Mr. Grobnik.

"Hard work builds muscles," Mr. Grobnik said. "Look at your mother. Strong like an ox."

So Slats went to a bowling alley to work as a pinsetter. But on the first ball, a pin flew up and hit him on the forehead.

When he came to, he had a large lump on his brow, and the owner of the place was frantically stuffing a dollar in his pocket and telling him to go home and forget it.

Slats crossed his eyes and groaned until the owner made it $3.

It was such a big lump that Slats decided not to waste it. He pulled his cap over his forehead and went to another bowling alley to set pins. On the first ball, he staggered up the lane, holding his head. He got $5 from that owner. And at the next place, he made terrible wheezing sounds and walked out with $7 and an ice cream bar.

When the lump subsided, Slats sighed: "Too bad. It was worth its weight in gold."

But he still wanted muscles, so he talked to his uncle, Frank Grobnik. Frank seldom worked, but he had a tremendous build. His stomach was enormous, the biggest in the neighborhood.

When patted, it made a sound like a kettledrum. He was famous for feats of strength in the corner tavern, such as lifting the juke-box and dancing with it.

He told Slats that the secret of his strength was that he never ate anything but pig's knuckles, hard-boiled eggs, and beer.

Slats tried it. The result was that he was home from school two days with a hangover.

That's when he discovered the Charles Atlas course. While thumbing through one of his father's magazines, looking for pictures of scantily clad women, he saw the body-building ad. He sent in the coupon, the instructions came, and the exercise began.

The Atlas system—known as "dynamic tension"—required no equipment. It consisted of exercises such as one arm pushing against the other.

One morning, Slats was exercising wildly. He was all tangled up, with his arms pushing against each other, his knees pushing against his chin, his elbows flapping, Adam's apple jiggling, chest heaving.

His mother happened to walk by his room, and when she saw him she screamed that whatever he was doing was a sin and would probably cause blindness.

But Slats kept with his exercises all through the winter. And when summer came, he flexed his right bicep for some friends. One of them squeezed it to see if it was a pimple and would disappear.

It didn't. Slats knew he was ready. He finally had a muscle.

The next Saturday, he went to the North Av. Beach and strolled around, flexing his bicep and looking for the girl.

Suddenly, he saw her sitting on a blanket.

"Remember me?" he said, kicking sand all over her.

She stood up, and Slats punched her in the jaw, knocking her down.

"That'll teach ya," Slats said.

As he turned to leave, two young men stepped up and punched him silly.

Slats sent the course back to Charles Atlas and demanded a refund. He didn't get it, even though he threatened to distribute pictures of himself in a bathing suit to show what exercise did to him.

A long time later, Slats admitted that he shouldn't have gone to the beach and punched that girl.

"It was a dumb thing to do," he said. "I should have waited until I could get her alone and punch her."

HOW
SLATS
LOST
HIS
CYMBALS

March 7, 1973

Many people were shocked by the story of the two baseball players who swapped their wives, children—EVEN THEIR DOGS. They see it as still another example of our new, loose morality.

That may be. But it isn't the first time such a thing has happened.

I remember a slightly similar incident involving the Grobnik family, who used to live in my old neighborhood.

The cause of it all was Slats Grobnik, the eldest son.

One day he decided to join the aldermen's marching boys band, which played in his parades and rallies and also threw stones at windows displaying pictures of his opponent.

The alderman had been Slats' hero ever since his father had said he never worked a day in his life.

Because of his peculiar ear for music, Slats was given the cymbals to play. He rushed home and immediately began practicing. He hoped that if he did well, the aldermen would let him play something else, such as the horses.

Mr. Grobnik was working nights at the time, so when Slats began marching through the flat, clanging the cymbals, he came roaring out of bed.

He hit Slats on the head with one of the cymbals, causing the boy's eyes to roll even more than they usually did.

This touched off a terrible row, with Mrs. Grobnik crying that her husband should not stifle Slats' musical development.

That was when Mr. Grobnik said he would like to swap his family.

"I would trade all of you for a little peace and quiet," he shouted, hitting Mrs. Grobnik with a cymbal too.

"Ma, you can get alimony," Slats yelled. "I will be your witness."

Mrs. Grobnik gathered her clothes and children and said she was leaving and would not return until Mr. Grobnik apologized.

At first, Mr. Grobnik could not believe they were really gone. To make sure, he changed the locks. Then he went back to bed.

Mrs. Grobnik took the children and went around the corner to stay with her friend, Ruby Peak, who had a nice apartment above the war-surplus store.

"Now you are the man of the family," Mrs. Grobnik tearfully told Slats. He turned pale, thinking that meant he might have to go to work.

Word of the breakup quickly spread through the

neighborhood. Naturally, some of the unattached women set their caps for Mr. Grobnik. They didn't get anywhere with him, though, because he didn't like women who wore caps.

The shapely widow who ran the corner bakery hurried over with some fresh sweet rolls for him.

And as Mr. Grobnik ate them, she leaned forward and whispered huskily in his ear:

"Is there anything else you would like?"

"Yeah," he said, "next time bring a loaf of rye."

When Slats' teacher heard of the separation, she worried that he might suffer a trauma.

The next day he came to class with tears streaming down his face.

The teacher assumed it had something to do with his home life. Actually, somebody in the schoolyard had told a filthy joke and Slats had laughed until he cried.

She put her arm around him and said: "There, there."

Slats said: "Where, where?" and gave her a pinch.

She ordered him from the room, which didn't bother Slats, as he figured he had learned enough for one day.

A few days after the separation, old Mrs. Novak asked Slats what his mother was doing.

"She is going to Reno," Slats said.

He didn't know what that meant, but he had heard someone say it in a movie.

Old Mrs. Novak didn't know what it meant either. She figured it must mean Mrs. Grobnik had run off with a man named Reno.

So she went to the grocery store and told all the other ladies about it.

"I'll bet he is a no-good gigolo," one of them said.

That afternoon, they all told their husbands that Mrs.

Grobnik was carrying on with Mr. Reno, a notorious gigolo.

The husbands discussed it in the tavern. One of them said: "I think I know the guy. He lives over in the Italian neighborhood."

Another said: "I know the one. He has a mustache and hangs out in the pool hall."

When Mr. Grobnik stopped for a beer, they told him his wife was in love with a notorious pool shark and fortune hunter named Reno, who had a mustache and wore pointy shoes.

"Everybody in the neighborhood knows about it," the bartender said. "I hear she has even sold her wedding ring to give him money."

Enraged, Mr. Grobnik went to the pool hall and punched the first man he saw wearing a mustache. He turned out to be a jukebox distributor, and three of his boys beat Mr. Grobnik with pool cues.

When Mr. Grobnik came to in the hospital, his wife and children were at his bedside. Mrs. Grobnik said she would come back home and make Slats give up the cymbals.

"Will you stay away from Reno?" Mr. Grobnik said.

"But Reno is in Nevada," said Mrs. Grobnik.

Mr. Grobnik smiled. "Good. I must have really taught him a lesson."

BEER BELLY'S GARAGE SALES

May 14, 1973

A tightfisted friend, in noting my column on the decline of bargain hunting along Maxwell St., has reminded me of another once-popular source of inexpensive merchandise.

It was the garage sale. But not the kind now held in the suburbs, where people sell their useless possessions in order to raise some money to go to E. J. Korvette's and buy more useless possessions.

The earlier garage sale was held when the word was whispered around the neighborhood that somebody had some ''stuff'' they wanted to unload. You did not ask where it came from.

A neighborhood with industrious young men had these sales often. As often as the young men could find an unguarded warehouse, truck, or store.

The one rule a shopper at such sales had to remember was to never buy anything bearing a serial number, which could be traced.

The man who held garage sales in our neighborhood was Slats Grobnik's uncle, Beer Belly Frank.

Basically, he was a gentleman of leisure. He spent most of his time in the tavern, eating hardboiled eggs and drinking beer. Or fishing for perch off North Av. Or managing the tavern's softball team, or going to Cubs' park. He knew how to live.

Once in a while he would work a day for the local furniture mover, but only if the job involved first-floor flats. And during the Christmas season he sold Christmas trees in a vacant lot. He was a master at drilling holes in the trunk of a skinny tree and gluing in branches.

But his furtive garage sales were the real source of his income.

Every couple of months or so Frank would let out the word that "a shipment was in." Actually, he didn't have to say anything. People knew "a shipment was in" because Frank would start wearing his dark glasses, a gray fedora, and would talk out of the corner of his mouth. At such times, he even ate and drank out of the corner of his mouth.

The word would spread through the neighborhood, with everybody talking out of the corner of their mouths, winking and looking sly.

Then on Saturday morning they would drift to the garage behind the tavern, knock, and Frank would open the door just a crack and give them a penetrating look.

Sometimes, to play it safe, he might ask a few questions.

Like: "Who are ya and who sent ya?"

The answer was usually something like: "I'm your sister and you sent me. Why don't you take off those dark glasses so you can see?"

In the garage would be the "merchandise," stacked on tables or hanging from nails in the wall. Most of the time it was new clothing—men's, women's, children's—everything from suits to socks.

The labels had always been removed. People would nod knowingly at this. They knew it meant somebody was taking no chances.

When they found something that fit, they would pay Frank at the door, stuff the garment into a shopping bag, and slip into the alley. In a hard voice, Frank told everybody the same thing: "Remember, you didn't get it from me."

Nobody was supposed to ask questions about the source of the merchandise, but once in a while somebody would forget and blurt out something like: "Is it really hot stuff?"

Then Frank would use his powerful belly to push the big-mouth against the walk, and he'd rasp: "People who ax too many questions get put in a sewer, see."

He always sold everything. That's because his "contacts," as he called them, managed to come up with clothes for the coming season.

In the fall, it was heavy jackets, long underwear, caps with earflaps, and maybe some gabardine suits. In summer, he would manage to obtain "a shipment" of T-shirts. And just before Easter, he always had a line of men's and boys' suits and women's hats.

One Christmas, he even came up with several cases of a perfume called "Moon Madness," which most of the men bought for their wives. The neighborhood didn't smell the same until the following spring.

Then Frank's sales suddenly ended. There was a rap

on the garage door, and when he opened it the police burst in with a warrant, accusing him of being a fence. Everybody figured the owner of the war-surplus store was the stoolie, because he had always complained that Frank cut into his business, especially in long underwear.

The whole neighborhood was watching when they marched Frank from the garage to the paddy wagon. Even though nobody had a camera, and everybody knew him, he held his gray fedora over his face the way the big operators always did.

Mrs. Grobnik wept. But little Slats was proud. It was the first time anybody in the family had been pinched for anything more serious than wife beating.

But within two hours, Frank was back. The men in the tavern were awed by his quick release. Even Harry the bookie didn't get sprung that fast, and Harry's father-in-law worked for the city. When Frank was asked how he had swung it, he snapped his fingers and winked.

The precinct captain was so impressed that he went to the police station to snoop around. He figured that maybe Frank should be an officer in the ward organization.

And he came back to the neighborhood with a shocking scandal.

The desk sergeant had told him that Frank had been released because he hadn't committed any crime.

The hot merchandise he was selling wasn't hot at all. He had bought it at wholesale houses on Roosevelt Rd., and had receipts to prove it. That's where all of his garage merchandise had come from, with Frank marking it up 20 per cent for his profit. None of it had been stolen. Not even one pair of long underwear.

That was the end of Frank's garage sales. For a long time, nobody would talk to him. And they never trusted him again. Not after they found out he was nothing but a big crook.

SOME
OTHER
FRIENDS

WHERE'S STELLA? A TIPSY TALE OF LOVE'S TRAVAIL

April 4, 1967

The most embarrassing thing that can happen to a drinking man is to wander into the city and become befuddled and lost.

I recall the case of a downtown businessman who had spent the evening out with some friends. He decided to stay downtown and sleep in his office, but he couldn't find his keys. He solved the problem by climbing a fire escape and entering through a window.

In the morning he awoke under a piano in a temple on Washington Blvd. "I could have sworn it was my office," he told a judge.

Something like this happened Monday morning to a

young man named George C. Thomas, who lives on 38th Street.

While having a few drinks, he began yearning for his sweetheart, a girl named Stella. So he went to find her.

A short time later, he was sitting on a sofa, bellowing: "Stella, Stella, where are you?"

This caused Jessie Barnes to jump out of bed. It caused Jessie's three small children to begin screaming. It caused Mrs. Barnes to grab a telephone and dial the police.

Barnes ran into his living room and turned on the light. George C. Thomas sat on the sofa and blinked.

"Who are you?" Mr. Barnes demanded.

"I'm looking for Stella, that's who," Thomas said.

"How did you get in here?"

"Through the window," Thomas said. Then he sat back and resumed bellowing for Stella.

"Shut up," Barnes shouted at his visitor and at his children, who were now almost hysterical.

Mrs. Barnes finished talking to the police and walked into the living room.

"Stella, it is you," cried Thomas, trying to rise from the couch.

"She is not Stella," Mr. Barnes said. "She is my wife."

"Got a light?" asked Thomas.

The conversation continued in this vein until the police arrived. Then it took them the better part of an hour to quiet the children and decide who should be arrested and on what charges, if any.

In court, later that morning, Judge Daniel Ryan asked Thomas to explain why he had broken into the apartment of total strangers and awakened them with the strange cry of "Stella."

Thomas, whose eyes were now pomegranate red, said:

"Like I told everybody, I was just looking for Stella. I love Stella."

Judge Ryan decided that Thomas was not a burglar, since burglars usually display more stealth, and had not intended to commit any harm. So he set Thomas free to go on with his romantic search.

The Barnes family returned to their apartment on Vincennes Av. They were in the house only a minute when one of the children ran screaming out of the bedroom.

Right behind her was a strange dog that had come crawling out from under the bed.

After booting the dog out of the flat, the Barnes family surmised that George C. Thomas must have had his dog with him when he crawled through the window. In the excitement and darkness it apparently hid under the bed.

I relate this story solely in the hope that it will be seen by Stella and that she will contact George C. Thomas so people can get some sleep.

ARE YOU REALLY A CUBS FAN?

The bookies say the Cubs are contenders for the pennant, so it must be true. And now the city is crawling with Cub fans.

But are they really Cub fans? Were they around, were they loyal, when everything the Cubs did was disgusting? Were they out there cheering when the only thing to cheer about was when the ball came off the screen and hit the batboy in the head?

There is one way to find out: If you are suspicious of someone, make him take the Cub quiz. It is guaranteed to weed out imposters.

Don't expect to answer many questions correctly even

92

if you are a loyal, old-time fan. It is hard. I made up the
test and even I can't get them all right.

Here it is: Five correct answers qualifies you as a true-
blue Cub fan and permits you to paste this column to the
front of your face.

QUESTIONS

1. What position did Max Stang play?

2. The fans in the left-field bleachers used to throw
packages of something at the Immortal Hank Sauer. What
did they throw? Keep your answer clean.

3. Name at least one Cub pitcher of the 1950s who
wore a golden earring.

4. The Cubs had a 38-year-old rookie in the 1950s.
What was his name?

5. Which current Cub swears the most?

6. What did the immortal Wayne K. Otto hit?

7. Which of these three players pitched a one-hitter
in the 1945 World Series: Eddie (Curly) Cronin, Greg
Czag, or the immortal Dicky Gongola?

8. Name two radio or TV figures who were once Cub
batboys.

9. The Cubs once had an outfield that was so slow,
they were known as the Quicksand Kids. Two of them
were Hank Sauer and Ralph Kiner. What pathetic wreck
played between them in center field?

10. Which of these two players always had sore feet:
Heinz Becker or the immortal Dominic Dallessandro?

11. The Cubs once had a first baseman who really
couldn't hit. Nobody could hit the way he couldn't. His
name was Kevin Connor or something like that. He was so
bad I still try to blot his name out of my mind. Anyway, he
became a TV star. What is his name now? (A tip: It is not
Kup.)

12. The immortal Lenny Merullo couldn't field or hit, and he wasn't fast. What was he known for?

13. Quick. When a ball goes over the left-field wall, what street does it land on?

14. Cub games are broadcast on radio station WGN. What station used to broadcast them?

15. The Cubs had a pitcher who was born in Ozanna, Poland. What's his name?

ANSWERS

1. None. He was Gravel Gertie, the immortal vendor.

2. Chewing tobacco, whenever he hit a home run or did some other heroic thing.

3. The immortal Fernando Pedro Rodriguez. He was undefeated as a pitcher in 1956. He also failed to win a game.

4. The immortal Fernando Pedro Rodriguez. You know, the guy with the golden earring.

5. It is a tossup between Ron Santo and Leo Durocher. Expert observers say Durocher swears more when he is angry; Santo, when he is happy. (This column is educational.)

6. Nothing. But Hack Wilson once hit him. He was a sportswriter, so he probably deserved it.

7. None. They were all my relatives and enjoy seeing their names in the paper.

8. The immortal Vince Garrity and the immortal Walter Jacobson. Garrity said he enjoyed being a batboy, except when the ball came off the screen and hit him in the head. Jacobson says he didn't like the job because players amused themselves by throwing their underwear at him. Now that he is a newscaster nobody throws underwear at him, but they should.

9. Frank Baumholz. He played in the mid-1950s, but

as late as 1965 or something he was seen lying in the grass in center field, catching his breath.

10. Becker had sore feet. Dallessandro had tiny feet. It used to take him 20 jumps to get out of the dugout.

11. Chuck Connors or something. I still can't remember, because he was such a terrible hitter.

12. He was best known for not being able to field, hit or run fast.

13. Waveland Av. But to hear Jack Brickhouse yell, you'd think it landed in his eye.

14. WIND used to broadcast Cub games. It's the station that used to broadcast the immortal Howard Miller.

15. Moe Drabowsky. Not only was he born in Ozanna, but he is still considered the best pitcher Ozanna, Poland ever produced. The best hitter from Ozanna was the immortal Ziggy Grobnik, Slats' father. He once hit his wife 12 times without a miss. But that's another game.

JOB-FIGHTERS
LOSE
LAST
HAVEN

October 25, 1967

Social workers are being sent into Chicago pool halls for the malicious purpose of persuading pool players to take regular jobs.

This is part of the federal war on poverty and it shows how dirty a war—even a poverty war—can be.

As a taxpayer I object to my money being used for such an inhuman purpose. Napalm bombs on villages are one thing. How can we make Vietnam free if we don't first burn it? But infiltrating pool halls with social workers is an atrocity.

Pool halls have always been off limits to certain types of undesirables, such as women, children, and preachers, and that is as it should be. The pool hall provides a sanctu-ary for men who want to escape creeping togetherness, one of the great dangers to our way of life.

Few such sanctuaries remain. Bowling alleys used to be almost as good as pool halls. Some of the most stimulat-ing conversation ever heard occurred when a wine-loving pinsetter and a beer-drinking bowler argued about whether the bowler intentionally threw a ball while the pin-setter's head was in the way. But now the bowling alley has become a family center. Instead of sending their children outside to play in the fresh air pollution, parents send them to kiddy bowling leagues before they are even old enough to falsify their ID.

Taverns long ago adopted the bad practice of admit-ting women, which led to the wall signs that prohibit swear-ing and other simple pleasures.

The pool hall alone has tried to retain its dignity and traditions. It's been difficult because of the emergence of the pseudo-pool hall, places that actually encourage women and families to enter and play. These are not really pool halls. They are simply public basement-recreation rooms.

So the pool hall has slowly dwindled in number. Only a few good ones remain in Chicago, simple, quiet places where men can gather to swear, lie, shoot pool, or watch someone else shoot pool, hustle or be hustled, read a scratch sheet, bet, doze, all without intrusion.

There is nothing like a pool hall, except maybe a steam bath, and there is not much to bet on in a steam bath.

The few remaining pool halls won't survive if social workers start coming around and bothering the players about going to work.

I don't even trust the motives of the social workers. Do they actually believe that pool players do not know that there are jobs available outside the pool hall? Of course they know it. It was the thought of working regularly that sent so many of them into the pool hall in the first place.

As the great Rudolph Wanderone, better known as Minnesota Fats, has often said on the subject of work:

"I ain't never lifted anything heavier than a fork, and I never will."

Or as the lesser-known Slats Grobnik, also known as Armitage Av. Stupid, has often said:

"If work is so good, how come we got rid of the 12-hour day?"

Fats would not have become a great pool player, thereby avoiding regular work, if a Miss Sally Dewgood was forever popping out of the corner pocket and nagging him about the filling out of a welfare form or taking a job in a bakery. His nerves would have been ruined and America would have lost a great athlete and an inspiration to youth.

I suspect that the social workers really don't care if pool players work. They are offended by the thought of happy, shiftless men surviving without their help. They want to inject them with ambition, upward mobility, stability, and other dread social diseases.

An American institution is in danger and the social workers should be stopped. We might not save the lake, but we can save the pool player.

Remember, there are 75,000,000 people holding jobs in the United States. But there is only one Minnesota Fats.

AH, LIFE'S SWEET MYSTERY

Bill Malloy, a Chicago folk singer, went to Vietnam some time ago to entertain troops.

After his tour, he traveled to India to fulfill an ambition. He wanted to talk to wise men. And India, as everybody knows, has always been known for its wise men.

Malloy talked to them about the meaning of life. This is the best thing to talk to wise men about, as they aren't much on football and politics.

But when he finished his travels in India and came back to Chicago, he still did not have an answer to the question: "What is the meaning of life?"

One day Malloy noticed the catchy slogan on the Standard Oil Service Stations signs:

"As you travel, ask us."

He wondered if this might be some kind of omen. If you hang around wise men long enough, you start thinking this way.

So Malloy became a Standard customer hoping to find what India could not give him.

Every time he pulled into a gas station, he would ask:

"As a traveler, could I ask you a question?"

"Yes sir, that's what our slogan is all about."

"What is the meaning of life?"

The attendants answered in many ways.

One said: "I'm new here."

Another offered: "I don't remember anything in the manual on that."

There was an attendant who said: "I'm not much for church, myself."

And one gave him a leer and a wink, whatever that meant.

Most, however, stared vacantly before cleaning his windshield, even when it was clean, which is meaningless.

Somehow, word of his persistent questioning of attendants got back to Standard Oil's department of customer relations.

And one day Malloy got a phone call at the Inter-University Center, where he works when he isn't singing to folks.

"We understand," the customer relations man said, "that you have been asking our dealers questions and getting unsatisfactory answers."

"That is true."

"What have you asked, may I ask?"

"I have asked them if they can tell me the meaning of life."

"Why do you ask our dealers that?"

"Because your sign says: 'As you travel, ask us.' "

"Well, you must understand that not all of our attendants are trained in metaphysics."

"That may be so; nevertheless you are guilty of misleading advertising because none of them can answer my question."

"We answer most questions."

"Yes, but I am not interested in a good place to eat, a good fishing hole, or a clean motel. I want to know the meaning of life."

The customer relations man thought about this for a moment. Then he suggested that Malloy write out his question and send it to Standard Oil with a self-addressed envelope, including his zip code number, of course.

"We will try to find the answer," he promised.

Malloy followed instructions and in a week he received a letter from Standard Oil.

His fellow employees crowded around, but Malloy went into his office and shut the door.

"I wanted to be alone at a time like that," he said.

He opened the envelope. Inside was finally the answer to his question.

It contained an application for a Standard Oil credit card.

Malloy said: "They gave me the only answer they knew."

A SALESMAN'S TOPLESS STORY

The man swears the story is true. I have heard stranger stories about Christmas office parties, so I believe him.

He is a salesman. Some time before midnight the party broke up. After a final ho-ho to his fellow workers, he strode into the night.

Before he could get to his car, a strong wind snatched his toupee from his head and carried it down a dark side street.

This usually doesn't happen to his headpiece, but after a long evening at a party everything gets a little loose.

A headpiece that doesn't look like it is worn for laughs—one that can fool some of the people all of the time—costs more than a few dollars. So he put his hand over his suddenly cold dome and hoofed down the street after it.

Trying to find a lost toupee on a dark street at night isn't an easy assignment. There was snow on the lawns, and in some places the brown grass showed through.

"I didn't realize," he said later, "how much a few inches of dry grass showing through snow can look like a headpiece."

So he loped along, stopping in front of almost every house to paw at the grass, then straightening up and moving on.

A policeman was driving by, and the salesman's behavior attracted his attention.

The salesman explained what had happened, pointing at his bald head and saying: "Look, there's proof."

"I advise you to go home," said the policeman, who had a full head of hair. Why should he care?

The salesman went back to his car, but instead of going home, he drove slowly down the street, trying to spot the lost object.

His luck was all bad. The same policeman noticed the slow-moving car and pulled it over.

"You again," he said.

"It is still lost," the salesman said.

A little while later, he was in a cell in a North Side police station, charged with drunken driving, and trying to think of a relative who might have $500 for bond money in the house on Christmas eve.

Such relatives are hard to find, so he spent the night in the cell.

In the morning, a wagon came around and took him to Holiday Court, at 26th and California.

This is a court where people are brought from all over the city, regardless of what they have done. A judge sets bond, and if they can post, their cases are continued so they can go home.

Everybody is put in a large cell—called "the bull-pen"—to wait his turn.

The salesman tried to make conversation with a brooding young man who sat next to him.

"Believe it or not, I'm here because the wind blew my headpiece off," he said. "What did you do?"

"They say I killed somebody," the young man said.

"I see," said the salesmen, who did not try to make further conversation.

Finally at noon, when the accused killers, stickup men, junkies, and other holiday revelers had their hearings, the salesman was brought out. The kindly judge set a low bond, so he went home.

I pass this story along, not to moralize about office parties, staying out of strong winds, or any of the obvious messages it contains, but for a practical reason.

If anyone on the North Side happens to find something on his lawn that looks like the top of a head, don't get hysterical. Just send it along to me with the location where it was found, and I'll pass it on to the owner. He wants to use it as evidence.

WHO ACTUALLY CREATES GAPS?

A student berated me recently for the failure of my generation to stamp out war, poverty, injustice, and prejudice.

He said we were do-nothings when we were his age. And because of us, his generation now had so much evil-curing to do.

I couldn't think of any excuses, so I just mumbled that I'd been busy and couldn't get around to everything.

But the truth is, I had never given any thought to being part of a particular generation, so I couldn't say much about its accomplishments.

That's a mistake. We must speak up for our own generation.

Unfortunately, I'm not sure what to say about it. There aren't many generations that were less exciting. I'm not even sure of its name.

It's the group that was born just before and after the Depression began. People who are part of it are now saying: "Forty? The prime of life."

If any generation had an inferiority complex, mine did.

For one thing, it was really small. Today's young generation is enormous because everybody wanted babies after World War II, and just about everybody had them.

Half the kids born in my generation were "accidents." That's a hearty welcome for you.

A Depression childhood left its mark. Maybe we were too young to have to scratch for a living, but everyone we knew did.

That's why we have different economic attitudes than the young generation.

They spend money foolishly and they enjoy doing it.

We spend money foolishly, too, and we enjoy doing it. But our stomachs hurt.

Then came the war, and everybody had a brother, uncle, or father in it. But as adolescents, we did nothing but collect old fat, old papers, old tires, and give dirty looks to neighborhood 4-Fs.

A few years later, our war came along. And those of us who took part were pioneers. It was the first time we took half a loaf.

But were we viewed as victims or martyrs? No. We were hailed as losers. Coming back from Korea, and expecting people to be interested, was about like coming back from a Wisconsin vacation with color slides.

Many members of my generation are still haunted by the question of why they did not rebel against their dirty little war, why they didn't march in the streets, burn draft cards, and all that. It was just as bad a war, and the women were ugly.

The question doesn't haunt me. I know why we didn't.

By then, the country was firmly in the hands of those who scraped through a depression and won a popular war.

Actually, they are still running things. But our young protesters are their children and they have become tolerant and understanding.

My generation wasn't their children. We were their young brothers, maybe, or their nephews.

I think they would have punched us in the mouth.

Besides, we were outnumbered. We were always outnumbered. Even in politics.

Today's young generation has had several political leaders they could follow, beginning with John F. Kennedy, and followed by his brother, and Senators McCarthy, Muskie, and McGovern.

We, too, had a forward-thinking, exciting, charismatic political figure. The trouble was, Adlai Stevenson kept losing.

Today's generation has even had its political villain in President Johnson. It could stand in Grant Park and chant an obscenity: "(beep-beep) LBJ," and feel good about it.

We had only Ike, and it was inconceivable that anyone could chant "(Beep-beep)" at Ike. We would have chewed on soap.

And so we slid comfortably into something resembling maturity, without doing a thing. At least, that is what the young student radical told me.

But you have to wonder where some of today's righteous movements would be without a few members of my generation—such as Martin Luther King, Robert F. Kennedy, Malcolm X, Lenny Bruce, all heroes of today's generation.

In fact, it makes you wonder exactly who is creating the gaps.

CHANGE
BUGS
AN
OLD
SQUARE

June 16, 1969

I walked past Bughouse Square the other night, and there wasn't a soapbox orator in sight. The little park at Clark and Walton was almost deserted. Only a wino asleep in the grass, and a pair of slim young men rolling eyes at each other.

It's the kind of change that takes place in a city without anyone really noticing.

Just a few years ago, original thinkers and plain loonies still went there to mount vegetable crates and loudly explain how they would reshape the world.

Since the turn of the century it had been Chicago's unofficial open-air forum for radical speakers. If your wife wouldn't listen, or if the bartender threw you out, or if you were mad at the world, you just got up on a box in Bughouse Square and yelled about it. Somebody would pay attention. Maybe they'd laugh, but they'd be there.

No subject was too touchy. On a good summer night, you'd have a choice of hearing about the comforts of socialism, the evils of communism, the cruelty of capitalism, the logic of atheism, the glory of God, the hell of war, the elusiveness of peace, the cruelty of bosses, the agony of marriage, and the certainty of the end of the world in 14 days or less.

Regardless of what a speaker said, nobody lobbed tear gas, and the FBI didn't take his picture for the files. The only punishment in Bughouse Square was being ignored.

It had all kinds of speakers over the years. Some sounded like they had staggered over from a nearby tavern. Others were as confused and vague as an alderman.

But there were real pros, often self-educated workingmen who lived alone and liked to research an offbeat subject at the library, talk about it in the park, and pass the hat for the price of a meal or a binge. In a way they were the professional ancestors of today's TV commentators.

Serious radicals from across the country made Bughouse Square a regular stop. Before both world wars, the park echoed with antiwar sentiments. Advocates of the labor movement were safe from billy clubs in the square.

Long before today's generation was born, soapboxers talked about hunger, slums, inequality, the draft, and giving poor people a voice in governing themselves. Audiences heckled and laughed when they listened to pipe dreams about the 30-hour week, social security, and free medical care for the aged.

The audiences were seldom as intense as the speakers. Most people drifted over because it was a good place to get an evening of free entertainment. Tourists liked it. They could go home and say they heard a dirty man talk about free love right there in a public place.

If the speakers were dull, which was unusual, somebody might be playing a washboard. And prizefights were held on the grass a few times.

Local Bohemians and intellectuals hung around the park, and they were fun to gawk at. It was something like an early-day Old Town, but without the gloom of today's youths.

By losing its voice, Bughouse Square has completed a cycle.

Originally a cowpath, it was given to the city by its original owner in 1842 to be used as a park. And for many years it was just a quiet little city park—formally known as Washington Square.

When it became an orators' haven it was dubbed "Bughouse Square." Now it is just a quiet little city park again.

There is no mystery to why it has stopped being Bughouse Square.

Who needs it today? The whole country has become "Bughouse Square."

THE OLD DAYS WERE LOUSY

It has been reported that a dozen or so men's hair sprays now are on the market.

The sprays are part of a huge grooming industry that revolves around the heads of young American males.

I don't know why all of the sprays, creams, oils, and other beauty aids are so popular. There have been only two hair products that were of any practical value and they aren't used much today.

One was Larkspur Lotion. The other was 5-cent-a-quart kerosene.

They did not make your hair glow or keep it in place.

111

Women weren't overwhelmed by the urge to bury their fingers in your tresses. They did not even make a person successful.

But they were great for killing lice. And it is definitely a social advantage not to have small creatures running around on your head.

This used to be a problem in many city and suburban neighborhoods. Not just in the poor areas, but in the lower middle class, the upper-lower middle class, the lower-middle middle class, and elsewhere.

A mother-son relationship included regular inspections of the scalp—touching scenes much like those seen in the baboon cages.

The most furtive scratch was enough to provoke an inspection. And this often led to the dreaded command: "Go to the drugstore and get some Larkspur Lotion."

In the more economy-minded households, someone would be sent to the gas station with an empty milk bottle and a nickel for a quart of kerosene.

Neither trip was pleasant. In the drugstore, the druggist would look understanding but other customers might snicker. At the gas station, there might not be other customers around, but the attendant probably would say: "Got 'em, huh, kid?"

During a real outbreak, half the kids from the neighborhood school might show up at the drugstore at the same time. School is where the lice were passed around. It took just one kid in a class to spread them. They had great leaping power. One could almost see them spring from head to head, across the aisles, up and down the rows of desks.

The chronic carriers were well known. Their names were uttered like curses by mothers.

"Stay away from Eddie, that pig."

"But he's my best friend, ma."

"Get a best friend who is not lousy."

The larkspur and kerosene were used in conjunction with a double-edged, fine-tooth comb. After the fluid soaked the scalp, the comb was used to rake out the dead or dying bodies of the foreigners. Those that still kicked were done in with a terrible snapping sound. No one who heard it can ever forget it.

The least fortunate kids were those whose parents were too economical or efficient to bother with Larkspur or kerosense.

You could spot them by their shaved heads.

A friend of mine recalls spending most of his childhood with a shaved head. He was a freshman in high school before he discovered that he had curly red hair.

"My father didn't go for the kerosene or the other stuff. He figured it was a lot easier to just shave me and my brothers. Then if he saw something moving on my head, he hit it with a rolled up newspaper. I think he sometimes did it just to let off steam. All I remember about those years was the whack, whack, whack of a newspaper on my head. But I was lucky. He was a cop and he might have used his nightstick."

The problem of lice seems to have declined. Walgreen's says it no longer carries Larkspur and has not done so for years. My neighborhood druggist says he does not remember when he last had a request for it. At one time he sold it in great quantities.

I don't know why the problem has declined. The federal government has probably made a study of it—if it could be found. The obvious answer is that people, including youths, wash their heads more often than they used to.

Anyway, it is good to know that there is an improvement on the outside of the head of modern man, if not on the inside.

THERE'S A REPLY TO THIS KNOCK

The thin young man coughed as he limped down the highway, past the rusting hulks of cars, toward the distant town.

Above him, the sky was a dark brown, from horizon to horizon. Brown dust covered the road, puffing with the man's steps.

On the edge of the town, he began looking in the houses. He would open a door, wait for a moment, then move on as if he knew what he would find. He found nothing.

Once he stopped and cupped his hand over his ear. He walked toward a faint sound, eagerness on his face.

The sound became louder and he ran around the back of a house. A gate swung in the wind, the hinge squeaking. He sank to the ground and sat a while, shaking his head and coughing. Finally he stood and went in the house.

In a pantry was a can of chili, which he pried open and ate. He held a pan under a faucet. A yellow fluid spurted out. It got darker, turning brown. He built a fire, and when the fluid boiled, and cooled, he sipped it, gagging, but forcing it down. Then he found a bed and slept.

Hours later, he awoke and went outside, looked at the brown sky, and limped down the road.

He was near the other side of the town when it happened. For a moment, he didn't believe it. He stood in the doorway just staring at the man sitting alone in a chair. The other man stared back.

"Can I come in?" the young man finally asked.

The other man grunted and shrugged.

"This is hard to believe," the young man said.

"What?" the other man asked.

"Another person. I kept looking, but I had given up hope that I'd find somebody else. I was sure everybody was gone but me."

The other man shrugged.

"Is there anyone else left around here?" the young man asked.

"I haven't seen anyone."

"Do you have any clean water?" asked the young man.

"No. But there's beer. I drink that. Help yourself."

They sat a while, drinking beer from the cans, coughing, and watching the dust blow past the picture window.

"I walked all the way from the East Coast," the young man said. "It took me months. You're the first person I found."

The other man grunted.

"I don't think I'll go any further," the young man said.

"It looks hopeless. And my chest is hurting more and more. It hurts all the time now."

The other man opened another can of beer.

"You should see it," the young man said. "The Atlantic is covered with a thick crust. I walked across the Great Lakes to avoid the dust. They were muddy in spots, but most of it has congealed.

"And in Wisconsin, I saw a sparrow. I stayed there for two days to be near it. Then it died.

"The big cities are gone. You know, I don't understand why everybody started dropping bombs when there was so little left anyway."

The other man grunted.

The young man started to weep. "I can't believe all this could have happened. How could the people have allowed it? What kind of insane men were running things? Why didn't the people make it stop?"

The other man stared at him for a moment. Then his eyes became slits and he spoke in a hoarse voice. "Shut up!"

The young man said, "What?"

"I said, shut up."

"But don't you care?"

"Listen, I don't like hearing people knocking the leaders. So why don't you shut up."

"But look what's happened to the country."

"I'm warning you. I don't like people criticizing this country."

"But don't you understand, there's nothing left?"

"Then why don't you leave it? Get out. Go somewhere else, and see if you like it better."

The young man shook his head. "But it has happened to the whole world, not just here. Everywhere. There's no place to go."

The other man leaned back in his chair. "Then if you

aren't going to leave it, you better love it. And you'd better shut up.''

Both men sat quietly, coughing and watching the brown dust swirl outside the picture window.

Then the young man softly said: ''Is there anything you would want to talk about?''

The other man thought about it. Finally, he said: ''You didn't happen to see the last Super Bowl game, did you?''

BATTLE OF SEXES GETS BIT ROUGH

December 23, 1969

When John Jolly comes up from Texas to visit the in-laws, he always drops in at Berghoff's men-only bar for some dark beer.

They don't have dark beer in Irving, Tex., and John Jolly loves dark beer.

Being a Texan, he also likes the relaxed, old-wood-and-leather, manly atmosphere of Berghoff's bar, a Loop landmark.

Not that he doesn't like women. He likes them fine. He even married one. But once in a while he likes to belly up to a bar and have a drink with the boys, " 'thout any women fussin' roun'."

So, last Thursday John Jolly excused himself from his in-laws and moseyed on down to Berghoff's, and was sipping dark beer and minding his own business.

It was a good feeling, kind of like those tall, lanky Texas wranglers must have had when they finished a long, dusty cattle drive and ambled into the saloon to wet their whistles.

Being 5 foot 8 and an accountant, John Jolly, 31, never punched cattle, but it was still pleasant sipping dark beer in Berghoff's.

John was on his third glass when the women came in. He stood there with his mouth open.

The women were the intense, straight-haired University of Chicago types. They were from the National Organization for Women (NOW), which is for total female equality.

They were there to protest the maleness of Berghoff's bar, and its alleged refusal to serve one of their members.

One of them had a camera. The plan was to photograph anyone who wouldn't sell them a drink.

The sight of them brought John Jolly's blood to a boil. There aren't women like that back in Irving, Tex. He felt like he was in the Alamo, with his back to the wall.

"I told one of 'em that she didn't have an American accent, and that she didn't sound like an American to me.

"Then this skinny fella who was with 'em, he had long hair like Jesus, he came in and he started talkin' to me and he almost had me convinced that I was wrong, and that they should be in there drinkin', just like they's men.

"So I offered to buy 'em a beer if they wanted one, even though the women were sure ugly.

"But one of them started to take a picture with the camera. Shoot, you shouldn't go in a bar and take someone's picture. A fella in a bar might not want his picture taken, dependin' on who might be lookin' for 'im I mean, you wouldn't go in a bar and ask a stranger his name, would you?

"So he started grabbin' for the camera, and naturally I stepped in to give him a hand. I figured we'd push them out of the bar.

"Shoot, somebody's got to stand up against this kind of stuff. It's a men's sanctuary. We wasn't botherin' nobody. I was just drinkin' my beer.

"Well, there was 100 men in that bar, but only two or three of us got in there and tried to push them out. Nobody wants to act.

"We started pushin', but all of a sudden these other women started comin' in from outside.

"Man, I tell you, they were huge women. I mean, they look like women wrestlers. They looked so mean I thought they was animals. I felt like I was being physically attacked.

"I got hold of this one, and I was holdin' my ground, and maybe even gainin' a toehold, when she starts chewin' on my hand.

"She sunk them teeth of hers right into the butt of my hand, below the small finger here, and starts chewin' like I was a five-dollar steak.

"I told her: 'Lady, you ain't much of an American, actin' this way!'

"I finally got my hand out of her mouth. Then the police came and there was a big fuss, but nobody was arrested or nothing like that.

"I wrapped a napkin around my hand and the boys at the bar greeted me like a champ. But why didn't they help out? They just stood around. They didn't come through in the clutch.

"I had to go to the hospital to get a tetanus shot. I was afraid I might die. That woman had a jaw like a wolf.

"Boy, I'll tell you this: If I had it to do over again, I'd bust her one good one, that damn, red-eyed female."

Mr. Jolly is on his way back to Texas by now. But he'll be coming back, and when he does, he intends to drink dark beer in Berghoff's again.

"It won't be the same, though," he said. "I won't be able to relax, thinkin' they might come through the door, their fangs showin!"

SAVE A KITTY FROM EXTINCTION!

Like many Chicagoans, I grew up with a distrust of most things and creatures, but especially cats.

The old women in the neighborhood always said cats were evil and were related to the devil. Some would cross themselves and mumble prayers when a cat approached. The only other creature they did this for was Slats Grobnik, who they said was even more evil than a cat, and not nearly as clean.

They talked about the terrible things cats could do, such as breathing near your sleeping face and using all the air, so you choked. When Slats heard that story, he moved his bed so he could sleep with his head outside the window.

And they told how cats were capable of mistaking your pulsating throat for a bobbing string and playfully plucking out your jugular. When he heard that one, Slats moved his bed back inside and slept for years with the blanket over his head, although the Grobniks didn't own a cat.

There were those who owned cats. Some even had two. They used them for chasing off mice, rats, and whatever else might come out of the wall.

But nobody in the neighborhood ever owned three cats. It was agreed that only a crazy old lady ever owned three cats. Even if a fat old man had owned them, he would have been considered a crazy old lady.

Now, through no fault of my own, I own three cats, and there are surely those who say I am a crazy old lady, which is not an easy reputation to live with.

It wasn't my idea. One of my issue, afflicted with a soft heart, brought them home one by one to save them from howling winds and deep snow. Even in July, that was his excuse.

Don't worry. This is not going to be one of those cute stories about what it is like to have three cats. I have a large dog that chases them regularly, and they spend most of their lives in hiding, so they are no problem.

However, now a fourth cat has arrived, rescued from the howling winds, deep snows, etc.

I was raised to believe that only a mad old recluse, who saved tons of old newspapers in the parlor, and concealed damp wads of money in rusty cans under the dusty bed, would own four cats.

Being thought of as a crazy old lady is embarrassing enough. I refuse to be pointed out as a mad old recluse.

So the fourth cat must go.

I could accomplish this by flinging it out the door. But that would put me at odds with the law. You may not realize it, but the Cook County Board just revised its animal ordnance. Any cat wandering around at night—even if it has an owner—is now considered an "outlaw."

Somebody should contest this unnatural law because, as the late Gov. Adlai Stevenson said, when he vetoed a cat-controlling bill: "It is in the nature of cats to roam."

But until then, I cannot defy law and order and send an "outlaw" into the night.

Of course, I could do as the neighborhood elders did when they had excess kittens or pups—put them in a sack, go to the Humboldt Park lagoon, twirl the sack over my head—and splash. The lagoon floor is littered with the tiny bleached bones of such unfortunate creatures.

But this, too, is against the law. Our meddling government has made it illegal for a citizen to fling any kind of creature—human or animal—into a park lagoon.

So I must take the only way out open to me.

A friend of mine keeps a tank full of piranhas, those little razor-toothed cannibal fish from the Amazon River. Admittedly, they are strange pets, and he really doesn't like them. It's just that his landlord won't let him keep a python.

He says I may, if I wish, throw my surplus cat into his fish tank.

I know this might offend kindly old ladies and sensitive children, so I'll tell you what I'll do.

I'll hold off feeding the cat to the piranhas for a day or two. It's only about three months old, and my friend says it could use some fattening up anyway.

That will give anyone who wants to rescue it from the snapping jaws an opportunity to take it off my hands. It is a Calico, by the way, and seems good-natured.

So if any little children happen to be reading this, you run to mommy and daddy and tell them they must do something to save the nice little Calico kitty from the mean man in the newspaper.

All mommy or daddy has to do is pick up the phone and call me at 321-2198 and make arrangements to get the cat before those hungry piranhas do.

Because if somebody doesn't, little children, it will be snap, snap, gobble, gobble, right down to his curly tail.

(I swear, I could write great TV toy commercials.)

A
POKER
GAME
TO
REMEMBER

The judge's clerk called out: "Everyone who was arrested at 4825 N. Kedzie, please step forward."

You could almost hear the bones creaking as they stood up and walked toward the front of the courtroom.

There was Sol Karsh, 72; Sol Rubin, 75, and Morris Sol, 77.

There was Sam Neurock, 82, and Sam Berns, 65; Harry Sternberg, 72, and Harry Winograd, 75.

And there was Leo Richman, 71, and Sid Lerner, 70, Max Feder, 60, and Louie Krandel, only 54.

They bunched together and looked up at Judge James

Maher, who is about 40. With their bald heads and wrinkled faces, they looked like newborn birds.

"Is the arresting officer here?" the judge asked.

Detective Tony DeRango said, "Yes, Your Honor."

The Sols and Harrys turned and stared at him. DeRango, a stylishly dressed young man, looked sheepish.

"Are you ready for trial?" the judge asked.

They looked at each other. Then Sid Lerner shrugged and said: "Sure, vy not?"

"Are you represented by counsel?" the judge asked.

All 11 heads shook.

Looking a bit concerned, Judge Maher said: "Would you like a postponement to get an attorney?"

Lerner turned to the others and they whispered among themselves. Then he shrugged and said:

"Vy should vee get an attorney? We're guilty, so vy do vee need an attorney?"

"You are entering a guilty plea, Mr. Lerner?" the judge asked, looking uncomfortable.

"Sure. Vee were playing a little nickel-dime poker in our club. It's a private social club. And vee play a little nickel-dime poker and vee take a dime out of every pot and give it to charity. So if it's a crime for old men to play a little nickel-dime poker in a club, ve're guilty."

The judge, detective, and state's attorney looked at each other in astonishment.

Judge Maher, almost stammering, said:

"But do you realize the consequences of a guilty plea?"

Lerner shrugged wearily. "So, tell me the consequences."

Judge Maher said: "You are charged with being the keeper of a gambling house. You could be sentenced to as much as one year in the County Jail and fined up to $1,000."

Lerner stared at him for five seconds. Then he shook his head and said, "Gambling joint? It's a social club, wit' 50 members dat pay dues and vee have coffee and cake and play a little nickel-dime poker or rummy, and I'm the recording secretary and all I do is keep the books on vich charities vee give the money to. Two-thousand dolluhs a year to Israel Bonds, twenty-five dolluhs a year to . . ."

Judge Maher cut in. "Yes, but do you want to get an attorney or proceed with your trial now?"

Lerner turned to the group and said: "You vant to proceed? Sam? Sol? Leo? Harry?"

"Are you holding a meeting of the club?" the judge asked.

Sol Karsh looked bewildered, but he smiled and said: "I plead guilty." However, Harry Sternberg shook his head and said: "I'm not guilty." So Sol Karsh said: "Then I'm not guilty, either."

Judge Maher seemed to slump. "Then the club is agreed that it will get a lawyer?"

Lerner looked at the members. They all nodded, except for Sam Neurock, at 82 the oldest and at 5-2 the shortest, Sam Neurock just smiled sweetly at the judge.

Lerner nodded. "We'll get an attoiney."

"Fine," the judge said, with enthusiasm. "Then I'll set the next hearing for Jan. 28. Is that agreeable to you?"

Lerner shrugged again. "Any day is OK. None of us are voiking. Ve're old, retired. That's vy vee go to the club."

As they walked into the corridor, the judge was shaking his head. The clerk began calling the next case from among the row upon row of policy runners, bookies, and all-around hustlers.

In the hallway, Harry Winograd also was shaking his head. He still wasn't sure how he happened to end up in Rackets Court on the 11th floor of Police Headquarters at 11th and State.

"I voik in a vegetable store near the club and I went up there on my lunch hour to kibitz. I wasn't even playing. So there's a knock on the door and somebody outside says he is looking for a painter.

"You see, it's called the Painters Club. Years ago it was for painters. Now it's just us old guys. We play a little nickel-dime poker, some rummy. We drink coffee and have some cake.

"Somebody opened the door and these two detectives walk in and say: 'Don't nobody move and leave the money on the table.' Big money. I bet there was $12.

"So they put us in the wagon, take us to the station, and everybody in the station is filling out papers and taking our fingerprints, and I'm trying to tell them I was just kibitzing.

"Then they put us in two cells. And we were there until 8 o'clock. Then a policeman who knows us came in and said: 'Hey, what have you got these old guys locked up for?' And then they let us out on bond."

His story was interrupted by Milton Kolman, an attorney, who walked over, shaking his head and laughing. "Listen, I'll take this case for nothing. Come on, maybe we can go back in there and get it over with today."

Harry's wife, Katie, said: "You will?"

Detective DeRango, who had been standing nearby, looked almost as happy at Katie.

"Sure," said Kolman, "it's my day to do something nice. Where are the others?"

The others were gone. They had already taken an elevator. But DeRango said: "C'mon, maybe we can catch them outside." Harry, Katie, and DeRango jumped on an elevator.

They caught up with them on the sidewalk, where a heated debate was in progress, with everybody talking at once.

"I told you vee needed an attorney . . . Well, whose

idea was it to plead guilty? . . . Listen, you shoulda told him how much we give to. . . . Den vy didn't you say something, smart guy?''

Katie shouted: "Listen, we have a lawyer upstairs. He says he'll take the case free." Detective DeRango nodded.

Sam Berns, who was angry, jabbed a finger against his own chest, and yelled: "I don't need him. My son-in-law is an attorney. I'll get my son-in-law. My son-in-law told me . . ."

"Yeah, where was your son-in-law when we needed him?" somebody said. They went back inside.

On the ride back up, Sam Neurock, the oldest and smallest, stood looking up at DeRango and smiling at him.

Sam Berns pointed at Sam Neurock and said to DeRango: "How would you feel if Sam dropped dead before January 28th, huh, how would you feel?"

DeRango looked down at tiny Sam's friendly face and slowly said: "I would feel terrible."

Back on the 11th floor, Attorney Kolman gathered them at the end of the corridor and explained the situation: He had looked the file over and was almost certain that the case would be dismissed for lack of a warrant, reasonable cause to enter, and so on. But they would have to come back on Jan. 28 because he needed time to prepare motions.

They listened closely. Then someone whispered: "Is he Jewish?"

They got back on the elevator. On the way out of the building they were still debating.

Katie Winograd, walking a few steps behind, shook her head, sighed, and said:

"My husband's buddies."

PRO
WEIRDO
OF
CHICAGO

There is somebody like Harold Rubin in most neighborhoods. Mothers tell their daughters to run if they see him lurking in the bushes.

Harold was still a young man when he picked up the nickname "Weird Harold." A girl called him that because of the things he suggested they do to enliven their dates.

Later Weird Harold became interested in photography. He liked to film nature scenes. At least he considered them to be nature scenes. But the police didn't, and sometimes they broke into the motel room while Weird Harold had his camera pointed at a writhing couple.

Harold reached a point in his 20s, with the arrests and

all, when many men might have considered talking things over with a psychiatrist. Instead, Weird Harold decided to make being weird his life's work.

Now, at 31, pudgy, his blond hair thinning, Weird Harold is probably this city's outstanding weirdo.

A while back, he ran a convention at a suburban motel for the mate-swapping set. Many people disapproved of the convention, but as Weird Harold said: "Nobody was killed at my convention. We didn't even have a riot. And isn't that supposed to be the main thing?"

More recently, Weird Harold opened his very own pornography shop—the dream of any weirdo—just south of the Loop. He may not be the first weird businessman in the downtown area, but he became the first to admit it when he named his shop: "Weird Harold's."

Pornography shops have become so common that they now feel competitive. Weird Harold's presence angered a nearby rival, Jerry Kavins, who opened his place a few weeks earlier in the next block.

It's hard to believe, but pornographer Kavins looks down on pornographer Weird Harold. He thinks Harold has no class.

"We are trying to make it a respectable business," Kavins says. "We want to take it out of the level of the peep show."

To achieve this lofty goal, Kavins, who is working on a master's degree in business administration at the University of Chicago, decorated his place in paneled wood walls, carpets, and has piped in music. Until you examine the books, you might think you were in the library of a private club. An elegantly dressed young black man sits with great dignity behind a glass display case that is filled with artificial sexual organs.

"Weird Harold," says Kavins with disdain, "has his place slapped together. His floors are bare wood. Going there compares to running down a dark alley and grabbing a dirty picture."

Kavins shakes his head. "How can a place like that make so much money?"

I almost sympathized with Kavins. Here he is, bringing all that high-class education and his suave manner to the pornography business, yet a scruffy person such as Weird Harold, who doesn't even have a degree, is doing better. It makes a parent wonder if there's any point in putting a boy through college. In fact, listening to young Mr. Kavins, I became convinced that education can be a complete waste.

The answer is probably that Weird Harold, like some fine baseball hitters and football runners, is a "natural." Pornography comes easy to him. He is dedicated to it. Kavins, on the other hand, would probably be just as happy selling worthless stocks or bad used cars.

Take the way the two of them acted when, shortly after I interviewed them, the police raided both their stores and confiscated their stock.

Kavins phoned, but he had lost his cool manner. His voice shook as he said: "Please, don't use my name in anything you write."

On the other hand, Weird Harold walked in with a shapely but vacant-eyed girl on his arm, and said:

"All right, City Hall wants trouble, I'll give them trouble. I'll haul them into federal court and get them for harassing me. My suppliers are backing me all the way. I'll open again as soon as I get new stock and I'll be even bigger. They aren't going to stop Weirdo. I've got big plans."

Pornography shops appear to be legally with us, at least until their novelty wears off among middle-aged men, their best customers, so you might be interested in what Weirdo's plans are for the future.

He says he will open a photographic studio in the rear of his smut shop, thus combining his two major interests. For $20 an hour, a man will be able to use the studio to photograph nude women in erotic poses. (Presumably, women will be able to photograph nude men, although Weird Harold says there has never been much of a demand.) Weird Harold will rent cameras, sell film, do the developing, and provide the females. The customer need only bring his cash and his fetish. It amounts to do-it-yourself pornography.

"They have studios like this in New York," Weird Harold says, "Why should we always be the Second City?"

Weird Harold, who claims to have his fingers on the city's, uh, pulse, says there is a tremendous interest in do-it-yourself pornography.

"Since word of my plans got out, I've had more than 180 requests for reservations for the studio. And not from bums. These are respectable people. In fact, that's the backbone of the pornography business. We don't let kids in, and it's too expensive for some bum. So our business comes from adult businessmen, professional men, people who are respectable. Why do they want it? How do I know? They have their hangups and I have mine."

Despite the proliferation of pornography stores in Chicago, Weird Harold does not foresee their spread into most residential neighborhoods and suburbs.

"Never. Somebody in a place like Skokie might want to buy this stuff, but they don't want us selling it in their town or anybody seeing them coming in. But they don't mind coming down here for it where nobody knows them."

Many people are probably alarmed by Weird Harold and his kind. He is disgusting, I'll admit. But he now operates his store in an area where there used to be a dozen or more strip joints. For $20 a young lady would retire to the rear with a customer. Now they are gone. All that remains are places like Weird Harold's, where they deal only in fantasy. In every way, we are becoming a nation of spectators.

A
WOMEN'S
LIB
VIEW
OF
POLITICS

Women's Lib has accused most institutions, including the news media, of being male chauvinist.

The news media denies this, of course, and says it treats newsworthy men and women equally.

If this is true, then by now we should have read stories about the two candidates for mayor that sounded something like this:

GRANDFATHER IN RACE FOR MAYOR:
OPPOSED BY YOUNG SINGLE MALE

Richard J. Daley, a well-rounded but fashionably dressed grandfather, today launched his campaign for an unprecedented fifth term as mayor.

In his first campaign speech, the 5-7 father of seven, pointedly avoided mentioning his opponent, lean, dark-haired Richard Friedman.

At a press conference, Daley outlined his reasons for running again, and was then asked if he thought a man could be a father and husband, while pursuing a political career. He said:

"Naturally, I'm a father and husband first, but my wife has always encouraged me to be a career man.

"I think people are beginning to realize that men are capable of doing something more than paneling the family room and changing the storm windows."

Daley, who combs his hair straight back, wore a crisp blue suit with ankle-length trousers. He said he would campaign on his administration's record. Asked if he felt that being a man gave him a special appeal to the male vote, he said:

"No, because I serve men and women, regardless of their sex."

Meanwhile, Friedman, who is single, lashed out at Daley's record, and at a press conference was asked if he had any plans for marriage.

"If the right girl comes along, yes," he said.

When asked for his views on whether a political career and marriage mix, Friedman responded:

"Definitely. I believe a man can be a husband as well as a politician, if he has an understanding wife."

Friedman, who has narrow hips and sinewy arms, disclosed that he often shines his own shoes and buys his clothes right off the rack. He said he owns six suits and, in response to questions from admiring female reporters, said he favors Old Spice after-shave lotion.

"To be honest," he said with a sparkling smile, "during the campaign I sometimes forget to splash some on.''

Both campaigners have tried to avoid being stereotyped as the "male" candidate.

Friedman, for instance, has refused to be photographed with his shirt off. And Daley has politely but firmly refused to flex his bicep for the cameras.

Friedman's campaign got a needed boost this week when he received a strong endorsement from Richard Ogilvie, the sandy-haired, plump governor of Illinois.

Ogilvie, the father of one, urged Chicago's Republicans to rally behind Friedman's candidacy, pointing out that the defeat of Daley would increase the chances for a 1972 victory for Richard Nixon, the wavy-haired President and a father of two, and Spiro Agnew, the tall, dimple-cheeked, crinkly-eyed vice president.

Friedman has indicated that one of his targets will be P. J. Cullerton, the petite, white-haired Cook County assessor.

The office of Cullerton, a great-grandfather of several, was the center of a scandal involving charges that favors were granted to politically favored real estate men, among them being Charles Swibel, the raven-haired, flashing-eyed owner of Marina City.

But most observers agree that Friedman has an uphill battle if he is to overcome the Machine and the vote-getting expertise of such Daley backers as Thomas Keane, a well-preserved grandfather, the statuesque Danny Rostenkowski, the pert and bouncy Tom Foran.

Political observers note, however, that regardless of the outcome, Chicago will be led by a stylish dresser. Daley has several times been named one of Chicago's Ten Best Dressed Men, and Friedman enjoys the youthful look. As one male voter put it:

''No matter who wins, this race will make people realize that we men can do something besides mow lawns or cook on an outdoor grill.''

RECORDS
FELL
BY
THE
MOUTHFUL

A labor leader summed it up best, as he stood looking out at the thousands and thousands of masticating mouths in McCormick Place Wednesday night.

He took a cigar from his mouth, shook his head, and in a proud voice, said:

"This is the greatest bash in the history of Man."

By now, most of the TV-viewing world—in other words, the civilized world—knows that this greatest bash in the history of Man occurred here in Chicago.

This is where 10,158 steak dinners were consumed under one roof. Nowhere in history is there a record of that many steak dinners—or any other kind of dinners—being consumed under one roof. In fact, there are few cities in the world that have a roof big enough to consume 10,158 steak dinners under.

The records that came out of this fantastic dinner are still mounting. It may be weeks or months before they are accurately tabulated and put into the record books where unborn generations will be able to read with awe of what Chicago's organized labor did to honor the mayor.

There are more records than the obvious figures of how many steaks, potatoes, fruit cocktails, chef's salads, crème de menthe parfaits, were consumed under one roof.

For instance, somebody has estimated that in eating the steak, each person made an average of 50 chewing motions with their jaws.

This means that 10,158 jaws, each making an average of 50 chews, accounted for more than a half-million chews, which is surely the most chews that have occurred under one roof in the history of Man.

And those were just for the steaks. When they are done tabulating the chews required to masticate the rest of the meal—the 10,158 potatoes, fruit cocktails, carrots, and more than 20,000 rolls—the numbers of chews will probably exceed 1.5 million—surely the most chews that have ever occurred under one roof in the history of Man.

Having observed it, I can assure you that there is nothing in the world that looks like 10,158 jaws spread over 3.5 acres of tables engaged in making more than 1 million chews.

(Incidentally, an early estimate is that there were 270,000 teeth involved in the chews. However, there is no way of exactly knowing how many of the teeth were artificial. But based on the age of the people at the dinner, it is safe to assume that these were the most artificial teeth

ever engaged in chewing food under one roof in the history of Man. However, an asterisk will probably go next to this record because it is only in the modern era that man has had artificial teeth.)

Then there are the number of Adam's apple jiggles (or bobs, if you prefer). These jiggles, or bobs, occur when you swallow.

Somebody has estimated that with the cocktail party and the dinner, each person averaged something like 75 Adam's apple jiggles. That comes to more than three-quarters of a million Adam's apple jiggles.

This figure does not include the jiggles that happen when people took an antiacid pill or just swallowed to choke back the emotion brought on by hearing the mayor make one of his speeches. If you include all of those, the Adam's apple jiggles will surely top 1 million, which is the most Adam's apples that have jiggled under one roof in the history of Man.

Naturally, the traditional belly-pats are being counted. Shortly after the meal was consumed, they began. Thousands of men, all over the enormous dining room—as big as two football fields side by side—sat back, smiled contentedly, or groaned pleasurably, and patted their distended bellies—usually twice.

For some reason, most people who pat their bellies to indicate that they have enjoyed their meal, do so twice. Once would appear to be a slap at the belly, and three or four or more would appear to be an indecent act.

So there occurred an estimated 20,000 belly pats among the men at the dinner, which is surely the most happily distended bellies ever patted under one roof in the history of Man.

Another remarkable statistic will surely result from the belts that were loosened. This occurred after the belly pats. Each man's belt was loosened by an average of one notch, or an inch.

That is 5,000 inches, or 417 feet, which is probably the most feet of trouser belt ever loosened under one roof in the history of Man.

There are the burps (an early estimate is 7,500); the "tttsssss" (that is the noise sound made when drawing a hiss of air between two front teeth to dislodge a particle of food). Early estimates are that 30,000 "tttsssssssssss" were performed, the most ever under one roof in the history of Man.

It makes a person feel good, knowing that it happened here in Chicago. And it makes a man proud to have a jaw.

A CHAMPEEN IS CROWNED!

It was almost 5 o'clock on Sunday afternoon when Jerry Murray and Sy Friedman walked out on the hot pavement and shook hands. The crowd cheered and both men looked sheepish.

This was it.

There are champions and championships. They swagger out of our TV sets every weekend.

But Jerry and Sy were about to compete for a championship that had never been before.

One of them would become the champion of the Chicago area in the manly skill of lagging a penny 10 feet to a line.

Being champion of Chicago is as good as being champion of the world, because in certain things being best in Chicago is being best anywhere—groin-kneeing, eye-gouging, ear-biting, dollar-hustling, or penny-pitching. New York is a rube town in such sport.

Both men started the day as part of a crowd of several hundred who came to Grobnik Field, which is usually a parking lot just north of where I work. Both lagged their ways through five preliminary matches until they were among only 28.

Then they lagged again and were among 14. And that is when it got tough.

You can watch all you want of the Wide Wide World of Sports. When you get down to Chicago's 14 best penny laggers, you are seeing athletes. Any muscle-bound goof can kick, throw, or punch something 100 yards. But it takes nerves, skill, and a cool thumb to lag a penny exactly 10 feet under excruciating pressure. I would say that any of the 14 finalists could take a brute like Dick Butkus in this sport of finesse.

By the final rounds, Murray was up against a mean-looking guy named Zatz. He took him and was paired against the immortal Harris Goldenberg.

This was a tough match because Goldenberg talks almost as well as he lags, but his mouth was still open when Murray hit the line with his last flip.

Friedman knocked off a hustler named Glick. Then he took on Pete Goschy, who lives on Oakley Blvd., and a college lad named Ned Gravel.

The ninth round came and the best four were left out of the hundreds who began. They were the kind who would tell you that a piece of WPA sidewalk is more elegant than a Persian rug.

Friedman, a studious man who used a slight crouch, was up against Ralphy Tyler, 22, stocky, wild-haired, and wearing a yellow T-shirt with the words "Joker Pub" on his big back. He was the sentimental favorite of the Greasers.

Murray, meanwhile, faced John Washington, a cool competitor who had knocked off favorites like lean Dan Suchanek, the best of the Southwest Side.

TYLER AGAINST FRIEDMAN

By the sixth lag, it was 3 to 3, and both players were tense and the lags were as much as eight inches off the line. Suddenly they began hitting within three inches of the line and it was 6 to 5 for Friedman.

The Joker Pub crowd cheered when big Tyler flipped a liner, apparently taking the lead. But Friedman, coolly put one even more firmly on the line for two points and an 8 to 5 lead that held up.

WASHINGTON AGAINST MURRAY

Washington, who had been wasting brilliant liners on easy, earlier opponents, found himself four or five inches short of the line on each lag. Murray was so consistent he could have made money at Division and Damen, and he couldn't be stopped.

MURRAY AGAINST FRIEDMAN

So there they were, battling for the Slats Grobnik Trophy, symbolic of supremacy in penny-pitching, and the Willie Hyena Trophy, symbolic of being nearly supreme in the same sidewalk hustle.

Murray was so nervous in his first six lags he wouldn't have been able to stuff a coin in a parking meter. You could drop a coin more accurately than he lagged it. Friedman was coolly flipping within eight inches of the line.

"How the hell did he get this far?" somebody yelled at Murray from the watching crowd. "I did better than that and lost two hours ago."

Murray glared at his right thumb and something happened.

His next lag was four inches from the line. Friedman's was right with it, but the referee measured and it was Murray, by the length of a gnat's thigh. 5 to 2.

Murray flicked his wrist again, and he was two inches from the line. 5 to 3.

Friedman threw to two inches from the line. But the crowd yelled when Murray was closer. 5 to 4.

Friedman hiked up his belt, a la Arnold Palmer, and laid in a perfect liner for two points. 7 to 4.

But Murray came right back with a near liner. 7 to 5.

The pressure started to show, as they both were well off the next lag, but Murray was closer. It was 7 to 6.

Both were sloppy again. But Friedman won the point. 8 to 6.

Then it happened, and who knows what makes somebody come on that way?

Murray was within four inches. It was 8 to 7. His next lag was within three inches, and he had tied, 8 to 8, coming back from a 5 to 1 deficit.

Murray had won it, and he seemed to know it. His lag stopped two inches from the line 9 to 8.

His last lag was almost as close. And that was the end of it. Murray was the champeen.

Nobody played out any options, brought in their agents to ask for a million dollars, called a press conference to berate the team manager, or announced their retirement at the age of 24.

Friedman got the Willie Hyena Trophy and the other 12 finalists got plaques.

And, of course, the Slats Grobnik award went to Murray. He's the man to beat next year, and he promised to be in shape when he defends his brilliant title. As he put it, when he took the trophy:

"I am proud to win this and I intend to pawn it and spend the proceeds on beer."

Slats would approve.

OUR
PEDDLERS
HAVE
IT
ROUGH

September 8, 1971

Times being hard, Ron Wiggin, 22, was not too proud to sell balloons for a living.

The first time he tried it was on St. Patrick's Day. He went out on Michigan Av., sold green balloons, and made a few dollars. He decided that until something better came along, he'd stick with being a peddler.

So all summer, he has been selling balloons, "Smile" buttons, and yo-yos.

However, it isn't easy to sell balloons in Chicago. You can't just go anywhere. The parks are a choice location, but certain people have a monopoly on the parks. You can't street peddle anywhere in the downtown area.

So Wiggin decided to concentrate on the Rush St. area, where a lot of people walk the streets.

Lately that hasn't been a good location, either. For reasons known only to them, the police in that district have taken to arresting peddlers.

It apparently doesn't matter that the peddlers are operating legally, complete with city license. They are being arrested.

Wiggin has been pinched twice recently, but both cases were thrown out by the judge because Wiggin clearly wasn't doing anything wrong.

"The second arrest," Wiggin said, "was a charge that I was selling balloons in an alley, which is illegal. Except I wasn't in an alley. I was in front of Butch McGuire's Saloon on Division St.

"The policeman told me he charged me with that because he had to charge me with something. I asked him why he had to charge me with anything, and he said the district commander didn't want us selling on the street."

That's an old story in Chicago. It's this attitude that has made this a difficult city in which to buy a well-made hot dog.

Everybody knows that the best hot dogs are those sold by small old Greeks from sidewalk pushcarts. But how often do you see a small old Greek selling hot dogs on the street? In most parts of the city, they have been pushed out by the police.

There used to be an old cripple who tried to make a living selling razor blades, pencils, shoelaces, and other such merchandise on the street around Lincoln, Belmont, and Ashland. He kept getting pinched, too.

Hardly anyone sells things on the street in Chicago, except some young ladies who stroll around the Near North Side. And they don't get arrested as often as some-one who wants to sell balloons.

In most civilized cities, all kinds of peddlers are in the streets.

In Paris, ladies sell bunches of flowers, men sell toys. Outdoor book racks are all over the place.

Strolling through Rome, you can buy fried sardines and squid.

In London, it's fish and chips, umbrellas, bouquets of flowers.

On the streets of Madrid, you can buy salted nuts and Spanish candy, in Amsterdam you can get fresh herring, and in most German cities sausage stands can be found everywhere.

New York has its faults and problems, but in one respect it is superior to Chicago. You are never more than a block or two away from a hot dog pushcart, and roasted chestnut vendors are all over the place.

There are only a few great cities in which street peddlers are almost nonexistent.

One is Chicago. The other is Moscow. They are both run in a very orderly way.

MARRIAGE NO FIELD OF DAISIES

A standard scene in the modern commercial and youth movie is the couple running hand in hand in slow motion, through a field of daisies.

Sometimes they run in the soft summer rain, or on a beach, while pulling a kite.

You may have noticed that the couple is always young, and I'll tell you why.

They would not dare portray a mature couple acting that way, because we would all laugh.

Any grown man knows that if he goes leaping and bounding in a field of daisies, he will get a sharp pain in his chest. Or he will be stung by a bee, or he'll step on a young couple and twist his ankle.

If you go running on a beach pulling a kite, pretty soon you'll have spots in your vision and collapse from heat.

That's why, for every young fool who runs through high humidity and a field of daisies, you will find fifty wise older men in air-conditioned bars.

This wisdom comes to mind as one considers the dangerous course pursued by state Rep. A. H. Caldwell (D— Chicago).

He is the politician who is out to give 18-year-old males the legal right to marry without their parents' consent.

He tried to ram this law through earlier this year. The Legislature passed it, but Gov. Ogilvie, who is not a daisy-field loper, applied a well-deserved veto.

Caldwell says he will try again the next time the Legislature staggers into session. He is determined that any sexually frenzied young man, who has tried everything else without success, be allowed to seek the final solution to his tension.

I don't know what Caldwell's motives are. Maybe he wants to please the new youth vote. If so, he is shortsighted. They may like him at 18, but when they are 30 they will throw him out of office.

Or it may be that Caldwell, like so many older people, is offended by the youthful morality of today. As one of my contemporaries enviously put it: "I had to get married. Why should they get off easy?"

Caldwell's primary argument is that a youth of 18 is asked to go into the military, but isn't allowed the freedom of choice to marry. Then the answer, as far as I'm concerned, is to draft older men. Why heap even more problems on the adolescent?

Instead of making it easier for people to marry, the legislators should make it more difficult. Marriage leads to many of society's most serious problems. Study the crime statistics and you will find that the most active participants in homicides are husbands doing in wives.

This proves that when people really get to know each other, they take up arms.

It would be more prudent to tighten the marriage laws, not only for 18-year-olds, but for everybody. A marriage license should be approved by a board of marital experts that would consist of the following:

A bartender who has worked nights.

A man who pays alimony and child support.

A commuter.

The applicant also should have to go through a cooling-off period during which he would spend a day as an observer in Divorce Court, drive to and from the Wisconsin Dells on a hot day with three kids in the back seat, panel a rec room, and spend a Saturday night watching home movies.

Rather than running hand in hand through a field of daisies in slow motion, he should be required to climb a sand dune while carrying a cooler full of diet pop, a bucket of Col. Sanders' chicken, and fresh diapers.

Instead of flying a kite on a beach, he should be required to kite a bad check on the grocer.

Few males of 18 are sensible enough to handle marriage. Those who are wouldn't get married in the first place. Thus, the very act of getting married at that age is proof that the kid hasn't got enough brains, or he wouldn't be doing it.

Marriage is a serious step, and that is the biggest thing to remember. It is so serious a step that many couples who take it never smile again.

CHARLIE WON'T FORGET NO. 47

Charlie Koza had to work Saturday night, but he saw that as no reason not to celebrate his 47th birthday.

Since he was working as a bartender in a place off Michigan Av., the ingredients for a celebration were handy.

Champagne seemed like the proper drink for the occasion, so he opened a bottle.

But the owner of the place didn't like Charlie drinking on duty and said so. Worse, he billed Charlie $12 for the bottle.

Charlie called him a cheapskate, and he called Charlie a bum, so in a few minutes Charlie was walking out the door, his last week's pay in his pocket.

Charlie, who is divorced, now had two reasons to celebrate: his birthday and his unemployment. He headed for one of his hangouts on Rush St., where he switched to scotch, then cognac, and finally anything else his eyes could focus on.

He was buying people drinks and they were buying him drinks, and he felt pretty good until a former friend came into the bar.

The former friend was an off-duty policeman with whom Charlie once made a $40 football bet. Charlie won the bet, which made the policeman angry. But the policeman paid him only $10, which made Charlie angry.

Since they were no longer friends, they made nasty remarks to each other, and Charlie got the idea the policeman might punch him.

So Charlie staggered out on Rush St., waved at a passing squad car, and said somebody was threatening him.

The policemen went inside, talked to their fellow officer, and pinched Charlie for being drunk and disorderly. Blood is thicker than scotch. Or cognac.

It wasn't even midnight when Charlie found that his birthday party had been moved to a cell in the Chicago Av. station. He yelled that he wanted to bail himself out, somebody told him to shut up, so he sang "Happy Birthday" to himself instead.

At dawn, they moved Charlie to the weekend court at 200 S. Racine, and shoved him in with the other drunks.

Charlie loudly complained that he had enough money to get out on bond.

The bailiff told Charlie, "Shut up, you drunk," and pushed him to the back of the courtroom. Bailiffs in weekend court are not the kindest men in town. They are political jobholders, and have included slum owners and at least one professional arsonist who worked as bailiffs on weekends so they would have authority to pack a gun and badge the rest of the week.

"I got bond money," Charlie said, taking out a roll of about $100.

That was a mistake. Several young men, who looked as if they might have worse habits than drinking, stared at Charlie's roll.

"Shut up and wait for the judge," the bailiff said, shoving Charlie to the back of the room into the crowd.

One of the young men gripped Charlie's arm and said: "Man, you give us the money or you won't leave here alive."

Another young man tried to shove his hand into Charlie's pocket. Another squeezed his throat.

Charlie yelled: "Help, robbery, help."

The bailiffs pulled him out of the crowd, bawled him out for making noise, but allowed him to sit in a cell alone until the judge came.

When his case was called, Charlie started to explain about his birthday, but the judge didn't even glance at him, and a bailiff said, "Get out of here, ya' drunk."

Charlie didn't think it was safe to leave the building, even in daylight, so he went downstairs to the police station and offered a policeman $10 to drive him to the safety of the Loop.

"Don't offer me money," the policeman said. "I could pinch you for attempted bribery."

"I just need a lift," Charlie said.

"This is not a cab company," the policeman said. "Call yourself a taxi."

"Do you have change for a dollar?" Charlie asked.

"This is not a currency exchange," the policeman said.

Charlie decided to risk finding a cab on the street. He went outside and started looking.

He hadn't taken 20 steps when he saw the three young men coming up behind him.

Charlie gave it a good try. He held the lead for almost two city blocks, but then his legs gave out, so he whipped out his money, held it aloft and yelled: "Here, take it."

They hardly broke stride, taking the money like a football being handed off by a quarterback.

A motorist saw it happen and asked if he could help. Charlie got in and they followed the three young men, keeping them in sight while Charlie looked for a police car.

He spotted one. But just then it pulled into a car wash. By the time Charlie got inside, the squad car was already sudsy. By the time it passed the air drier, the young men were gone.

But Charlie didn't give up. He went back to the courtroom, hoping to get the names of the young men from the court records.

The bailiff said: "Beat it, ya' drunk, or I'll have you locked up."

Charlie went back to the police station, told a policeman about the way his birthday had turned out, and the sympathetic policeman gave him 50 cents for bus fare. It was his only birthday gift.

While he waited for a bus, he got caught in the rain and his suit was soaked.

Happy birthday, Charlie. And many happy returns. But next year, stick to cake.

THE
OLD
MAN
AND
THE
FARM

The old farmhouse stood along a winding, dirt, back road. It was the last house before the road disappeared into the heavy Wisconsin forest.

Except for a light in the house, the farm might have been deserted. Stacks of wood, boards, logs, railroad ties, and crates were everywhere in the yard. The machinery and tools were old and appeared unused.

But a light was in the window, and on a fence post was nailed a hand-lettered cardboard sign offering "Fresh honey."

The only animals in the yard were a friendly dog that

trotted to the car, and a cat that sat atop a pile of lumber and stared.

A minute passed, then the door of a shed opened and an old man came out. He was short, almost dwarf-like, and built so squarely he seemed to have no neck. His overalls were the color of tree bark, and a shapeless old work cap was pulled over his brow.

He walked heavily, with his arms hanging at his sides like a football lineman. "You want honey?" he asked in a thick Slavic accent. "Come in house."

The steps led to an enclosed porch in which more wood was stacked, and into the kitchen.

An old, black, wood-burning kitchen stove stood in the corner of the room. The oak table could have been as old as the house.

An old woman sat dozing in a wheelchair in the living room.

"He wants honey," the old man said. The old woman nodded.

The man pulled a chair from the table and said, "Sit." Then he opened a cabinet. The shelves were filled with jars of all sizes and shapes, old coffee jars, jam jars, all filled with honey.

"How many you want? Two?" He brought out two quarts.

How much? I asked.

He shrugged. "Two dollar."

He took the two bills, laid them in the center of the table, and sat down. "Where you come from?" he asked. "Chicago, huh? Is work in Chicago? Is peoples got work? Good."

He looked at the dollar bills, smiled, and said: "You have drink with me, huh?"

From under the sink he brought out a bottle of vodka, and carefully poured two shots.

He downed his drink, put the bottle back, and sat down again.

"Chicago, huh?" he said, pronouncing it shee-kah-goh. "Long time ago, I go Chicago. No more now. Too far go. I'm too old go Chicago."

How old are you? I asked.

"I'm 86 now. Too old to work farm, too. Now I take care of bees, sell honey."

"The farm, how long did you work the farm?"

He thought for a moment. "I came here in 1912. I buy 80 acres, all woods, big rocks. I cut down trees by myself. Cut up wood, chop up wood, take in wagon and sell to brewery. I clear all 80 acres, me and wife. Nobody around here then."

You came to northern Wisconsin from Europe?

He shook his head. "No. I come from old country in 1900. No work in old country. My father, he work 15 hours a day for 90 cents. Nothing to eat, no work.

"In 1900 I leave old country and go to Pennsylvania. Work in coal mines. Twelve years I work in coal mines. I save money, and in 1912 I come here and buy 80 acres for $800."

And there he stayed for almost 60 years. Now, he said, all of the original 80 acres, except the house and yard, have been sold for a modest sum. Small farms in northern Wisconsin aren't selling for much. Few people want to work as hard as one must to make a living from it. His sons have grown and gone to cities to find jobs.

A cold drizzle was starting to ride in on a north wind. He put some more wood into the black stove and moved the coffee pot over the heat.

Then he walked slowly back to the car and held out his hand. I've never seen a hand quite like it. The fingers were so stubby, they all looked like thumbs. The hand was dark and calloused from the wrist to the cracked nails.

"You got regular work in Chicago?" he asked. "You got steady job? Good. That's good. What you do?"

I told him I worked for a paper.

He nodded. "Good. Every day you work, huh? Regular work. Good. Is that hard work on newspaper? Hard work?"

I told him that I used to think it was. But not anymore.

$85
UNION
DEBT
WRECKS
CAREER

October 28, 1971

A study of the careers of two Chicagoans:

First, Ronald G. Becker, age: 35; occupation, sheet-metal worker.

Becker decided when he was a teen-ager that college wasn't for him, so he settled for a solid trade.

He went to Washburne Trade School, served his apprenticeship, and finally got his journeyman's card.

He made good money, and he needed it. Becker married young and he and his wife, Mary, have seven children.

Because of the size of his family, it took Becker a long time to round up a down payment for a house. But last year he finally got it and they moved into a three-bedroom home at 1212 W. 98th St.

Then Becker did something really dumb.

He neglected to pay his union dues. He got behind about $85. He says he was short of money.

So last January, he was suspended from the union and this cost him his job.

As soon as he was suspended, Becker arranged to borrow the money—including $815 to pay the union's initiation fee over again.

He says he got in touch with William Rooney, the union's secretary-treasurer, and offered to pay in full.

But he says Rooney told him he had to wait until the February meeting of the union's board, and the matter would be taken up.

He waited, but the board met and nothing was done. So Rooney told him to wait until the March meeting.

March came, but the meeting was canceled. Rooney told him not to worry, that the board would meet again in April.

Meanwhile, Becker's bills were piling up. He borrowed from friends to get by. The electricity was turned off once. The food budget was cut to the bone.

And Becker kept asking Rooney if he couldn't please pay his back dues and the initiation fee. Rooney, he says, told him to wait for the board to act.

In April, the board met. And they told Becker he should talk to Rooney. He did, and Rooney told him he was out, expelled, finished, all washed up.

Becker didn't give up. He went to the Legal Aid Bureau and asked for help.

A lawyer there called the union's lawyer, to ask for compassion. It took him three weeks of leaving phone messages before he got through to the union lawyer.

The union lawyer said he'd look into the case. Six weeks went by, and the Legal Aid lawyer repeatedly called the union lawyer. But he never got through to him, or had his calls returned.

Finally, the Legal Aid lawyer told Becker he'd have to drop the case because he couldn't even talk to the union lawyer.

Now Becker drives a cab ten hours a night and looks for work during the day. He's having a hard time finding a job because sheet-metal work is his only skill.

He has been earning just about enough to pay the food bill of his big family, and nothing more. He is three months behind in his mortgage payments, and expects to lose his house. The phone has been disconnected. The kids' $600 tuition at St. Margaret of Scotland School, 98th and Throop, is unpaid, so the kids will probably be transferred to public schools.

After 14 years as a sheet-metal worker, he is no longer allowed to practice his trade. For $85, he is banned for life.

That's one career. Now for the other.

Michael Daley, age: 28, profession: lawyer.

At an early age it was decided that Michael Daley would become a lawyer, like his famous father, Richard J. Daley.

He went to St. Ignatius High School, the finest Catholic school in the city, and Loyola School of Law.

Because he received student deferments, then later joined a weekend reserve unit, his law studies were not interrupted by the military.

And a couple of years ago, Michael Daley entered private practice.

Although he was not an especially brilliant student, Michael Daley has had a wonderfully successful law career. The firm of Daley, Reilly and Daley (his brother, Richard M.) has all the clients it can handle.

It is not surprising that the firm should be prospering. The name Reilly is magic in Chicago.

One of Michael Daley's clients is the Sheet Metal

Workers Union, Number 73. He will not say whether any other unions give him their law business. Unions are, of course, his father's most faithful political backers.

When we called Michael Daley to discuss the case of Ronald G. Becker with him, he was too busy to talk. He had a conference to attend. Later he was too busy to return any phone calls.

Therefore, we were unable to find out why he couldn't find time for more than two months to talk to a Legal Aid lawyer about Ronald Becker's expulsion from the union.

We didn't even get a chance to ask him if he had ever driven a cab during the night and looked for a job during the day, while worrying about feeding seven kids.

If we had been able to talk to him, we might have broadened the conversation to such fascinating subjects as how much his law firm is paid by the union each year— more than Becker now earns driving a cab, I'll wager.

We might have even discussed the bewildering paradox of big unions, and how they will provide huge defense war chests when their top men are caught stealing from pension funds, lavish fat pensions on union bosses while tossing a guy like Becker out of his life's work over a lousy $85.

We might have even asked how much the sheet-metal union has kicked in to his daddy's campaign funds over the past 16 years. If we knew that, we might be able to figure out how much of Becker's union dues went for this purpose.

But he's a busy young man, and has no time to discuss a nobody like Becker.

It's wonderful how quickly a man can rise only two years out of school.

And depressing how far another man can plunge ten years after apprenticeship.

CLYDE: A HERO WHO CHANGED

It was a long time ago, October of 1944. So long ago that the sons and daughters of the young men who fought in that war are voting now.

Clyde Choate was just a guy with four stripes on his battle fatigues back then, hoofing through Germany, a long way from the drawl, the coal mines, and the breakfast grits of southern Illinois.

If the German tank had turned the other way, swerved left or right, Choate might have gone through life selling used cars, his immediate postwar trade.

But it didn't. It came right at him, with infantry behind, overrunning his position.

Maybe it was fear, hysteria, numb courage, or whatever makes a man come out with guns blazing, but Choate came out with guns blazing.

First he ran forward and used a bazooka to blast the tank motionless. Then he came back and blew the turret off.

When the enemy jumped out, he drew his pistol and killed two of them. Then he climbed up on top, dropped a grenade inside, and got the rest.

Bloody, yes. But at that time, in that war, it seemed like the thing for a young man to do.

So they pinned a Medal of Honor on S. Sgt. Clyde Choate, of Anna, Ill.

There is no other honor in America quite like it. Play in the World Series, become the heavyweight champ, or Miss America, or even win an Oscar. That medal is, or at one time was, the great distinction.

Sgt. Alvin York won it. If we believe the Gary Cooper portrayal, he clucked like a turkey and the curious Germans stuck their heads up over the trench.

Audie Murphy won it, too, and if we believe his portrayal he mowed down everyone in sight.

Back in 1944 it meant something, and Choate got one. And Choate came back to small-town Illinois and got a job selling cars.

And that's when things went wrong.

How nice it would have been if he had kept selling cars.

But with that medal, the big one, the Oscar, the Most Valuable Player Award, you don't go through life selling cars.

Within a year, he ran for public office. And, the next thing you know, Clyde Choate, hero, became Clyde Choate, politician.

He joined the nondescript city hacks and Downstate

yahoos that comprise the majority in the Legislature. They gather in Springfield to chomp steaks, swill booze, listen with slack-jawed greed to lobbyists, and goof up this state worse than an invasion of crawling catfish.

Choate's medal did it for him and to him. Had the tank gone right or left, he would not have had the lapel pin that won his first office and made him the protégé of Paul Powell.

But it came right at him, so he became Powell's protégé. It wasn't too many years before he stood up in the Legislature, where Abraham Lincoln once served, and said of Powell:

"He stands as tall as the hills of southern Illinois stand above the river."

Powell became his political daddy. When ol' Paw Pal, as they say it Downstate, cast a vote, Clyde Choate cast his the same way. Like Powell, he described himself as an "ol' country boy." How the big-city lobbyists love the ol' country boys.

Now Powell is gone, and his epitaph is a hodge-podge of jokes about shoe boxes.

But Clyde Choate stays on. Today he is one of the wheeler-dealers in the Legislature, a big man from the turtle ponds of Downstate Illinois.

His clean-cut staff sergeant features have given way to the puffy-eyed look of the capitol politician.

The words of his army citation aren't nearly as well known as the words of his preposterous amendments to ethics bills, amendments aimed solely at killing any and all ethics legislation.

And his honored medal is mentioned only when he runs again, and again, and again.

He's far better known now for the thousands of shares of racetrack stock he somehow obtained.

That racetrack stock. Powell owned some. The

mayor's old law partners owned some. The ex-governor owned some. Some of our best-known politicians, Democrats and Republicans, owned some. It is the mark of being an influence peddler.

Most of the men who own racetrack stock weren't much better without it. Their backgrounds are nothing but hustling for the vote.

But Choate had that one day, when the bands played and the general pinned the medal on his chest that meant he, in his time and place, was one of the truly brave ones.

Maybe we ought to give our heroes big pensions that entitle them to a life of ease. It's embarrassing to see one of them turn out to be just another hustler.

HOW
TO
KICK
A
MACHINE

November 15, 1971

The guy in front of me put his dime in the coffee machine. The cup dropped, the machine whirred, but nothing came out.

He muttered, then started to walk away looking dejected and embarrassed. That's the way many people react when a machine doesn't come through: as if they have been outwitted. They feel foolish.

"Aren't you going to do anything about it?" I asked.

"What's there to do?"

What a question. If he had gone in a bar and ordered a beer, and if the bartender had taken his money but not given him a beer, he'd do something. He'd yell or fight or call the police.

But he let a machine cow him.

"Kick it," I said.

"What good will that do?" he said.

"You'll feel better," I said.

He came back and got in position to kick it, but I stopped him.

"Not like that. You are going to kick it with your toe, but you can hurt yourself that way. Do it this way."

I stepped back and showed him the best way. You use the bottom of your foot, as if you're kicking in a bedroom door.

I stepped aside, and he tried it. The first time he used the ball of his foot. It was a weak effort.

"Use more of the heel," I suggested.

That did it. He gave it two good ones and the machine bounced. He has big feet.

"With feet like that," I told him, "you could knock over a sandwich machine."

He stepped back looking much more self-confident.

Somebody else who had been in line said: "I prefer pounding on it. I'll show you."

Leaning on it with his left hand, he put his forehead close to the machine, as if in deep despair. Then he pounded with his clenched fist.

"Never use the knuckles," he said, "because that hurts. Use the bottom of the fist, the way you'd pound on the table."

"Why just one fist?" someone else said. "I always use two."

He demonstrated, standing close to the machine, baring his teeth, and pounding with both fists, as if trying to break down a bedroom door with his hands.

Just then, another guy with a dime stepped up. Seeing us pounding on the machine, he asked: "Is it out of coffee?"

We told him it had shorted on a cup.

He hesitated, then said: "Sometimes it only skips one, then it works OK."

"It's your money," I told him.

He put in his dime, the cup dropped, the machine whirred, and nothing came out.

All he said was "Hmm," and started to walk away.

"Why don't you kick it?" I said.

He grimaced. "It's only a dime."

Only a dime? I don't know anyone who hasn't been cheated by a machine at least once—usually a lot more than once.

First it was the gumball machine, taking your last penny. Then it was the gum machine on the L platform. Then the peanut machine.

And now they all do it. Coffee machines, soft-drink machines, candy machines, sweet-roll machines, sandwich machines.

Only a dime? There are 200 million Americans. If each of us is taken for a dime, that adds up to $20 million.

And it has to be more, now that machines have appeared in every factory and office, depot and terminal.

I once lost an entire dollar to a dollar-changing machine. I gave it five kicks, and even that wasn't enough. For a dollar, I should have broken a chair over its intake slot.

If everyone in the country is taken for a dollar, as I suspect we all will be eventually, that's $200 million. The empty cup is a giant industry.

Putting up a note, as many people do, saying, "This machine owes me a dime," does little good. The men who service them always arrive before you get to work, or after you leave. They are ashamed to face the people they cheat.

You can put up a note saying, "Out of Coffee," which saves others from losing their dimes. But that doesn't get your dime back.

The answer is to kick and punch them. If you are old,

lame, or female, bring a hammer to work with you, or an ax.

I feel better, having got this off my chest. But my foot still hurts.

ROCKNE
THROWN
FOR
LOSS
BY
FANS

It's become harder and harder to find movies that the entire family can see.

Even in those films that are rated as acceptable for everyone, a mammary or a buttock is liable to flash across the screen.

In some neighborhoods, the theaters have abandoned conventional films and have switched to the 16-mm. pornography shows.

I have never seen one because a long time ago Father Lawler warned me about what pornography can do to a man, and I surely do not want to be turned into a panting,

173

raging beast, prowling the streets in search of innocent young ladies.

But those who have seen them tell me that the performers do things that are not taught at drama school.

So people stay home and watch TV because there isn't a decent movie they can go to. Ask anyone why they no longer go to the movies, and they will tell you the same thing: There are so few "family" movies. And they will all tell you that if there were family movies, they would go.

Out in the Austin neighborhood, though, the people decided to do something about it.

They had seen one of their local theaters, the Rockne, at 5825 W. Division, slowly drift away from the family film.

It began in 1967, when Arthur Ehrlich bought the place. At first he showed the usual "G" rated movies. Then some "GPs," which are a bit racier. Then he brought in some "R" movies, which can make some people gasp.

And in July of this year, to use the phrase of the more modest generation, Ehrlich went all the way. He began showing those 16-mm. films, which have actual scenes of you-know-what.

People in the neighborhood were outraged and they organized against him.

Pickets showed up outside the theater, waving signs that said that they did not want movies in which people engaged in you-know-what, and demanded good family films.

Ehrlich ignored them for a while.

But leaders of the Northwest Austin Council stomped into his office and demanded that he change his policies.

So Ehrlich did. He agreed to family movies.

He also agreed to cut his prices from $3 to $1.25 for adults and .75 for kids.

He even threw in something extra. For $10 a month, an entire family could go the movies once a week.

That is a good deal. A family of five would be paying about 50 cents a person.

He offered the special monthly rate after the community organization said it would give him a list of 2,200 families that wanted to see family films and would go to his theater.

The community organization told him that at least 700 of the 2,200 families on the list wanted to buy the $10 monthly tickets.

All of this took time, of course. Ehrlich had to send applications to all the families. He had to line up some good movies and get his advertising ready.

But last week, decent, clean movies finally returned to the Rockne Theater.

His first double-feature was "A Man Called Horse" and "Little Big Man," both of which received excellent reviews when they first came out.

They replaced a couple of 16-mm. films called "Flossie" and "Wild Finish," which contained scenes that I would not even discuss with my old first sergeant.

This all proves, once again, what a community can accomplish if it organizes and people work together.

One other thing: You might be interested in knowing how business has been at the Rockne since Friday, when the new policy began.

Lousy.

On Friday, 247 people showed up. The previous Friday, 570 had watched pornography.

On Saturday, 354 people were there, compared with 530 the previous Saturday.

Sunday was better. The family fare attracted 423 people. That was an improvement over the previous Sunday when 338 turned up. Apparently pornography fiends rest on Sunday.

On Monday, the family double-feature drew only 51

people. The previous Monday, the antics of Flossie were seen by 212 pairs of bulging eyes.

And that special $10 monthly pass? So far only 93 have been sold.

At this rate, Ehrlich says, he will go broke.

But he is going to see it through the rest of the month, during which he expects to lose $10,000.

After that, though, it will again be X-rated movies.

"We've made the move," Ehrlich said. "Now where are all the people? What do people want?"

What do they want?

You know what? I think they want you-know-what.

"PATRIOTISM"
AT
THE
STADIUM

January 3, 1972

Both teams were on the field. The crowd stood for the singing of the National Anthem.

Everybody except one man. He just sat and studied his program.

The band began playing. The singing was led by a TV star who had been up all night drinking gin. Ten jets swooped over the stadium. Fifty majorettes thrust out their chests.

The one man stayed in his seat and looked at his program.

Somebody gave him a nudge. He ignored it.

"Stand up," somebody else hissed.

"I'll stand for the kickoff," the man said.

Another man glared at him. "Why don't you stand and sing?"

"I don't believe in it," he said.

The other man gasped. "You don't believe in the National Anthem?"

"I don't believe in singing it at commercial events. I wouldn't sing it in a nightclub, or in a gambling casino, and I won't sing it at a football game."

A man behind him said: "What are you, a damn radical?"

He shook his head. "I'm not a stadium patriot."

"I'll make you stand up," a husky man said, seizing his fleece collar.

They scuffled and struck each other with their programs. Somebody dropped a hip flask.

"What's wrong?" people shouted from a few rows away.

"A radical insulted the anthem," someone yelled.

"I did not," the man yelled. "I won't be a stadium patriot."

"He says he's not a patriot," somebody else roared, swinging a punch.

A policeman pushed through. "What's going on here? Break it up."

People yelled: "He insulted the flag . . . He refused to stand. . . . He's radical . . . Sit down—I can't see the girls . . ."

The policeman said: "Why wouldn't you stand?"

"Not at a football game," the man said.

"Hear that?" someone yelled, shaking a fist.

"Let's go, fella," the policeman said, leading him away.

He was fined $25 for disorderly conduct, and the judge lectured him on his duties as a citizen.

The next week he had a seat for the Stupendous Bowl game.

Both teams took the field and the crowd rose for the National Anthem. They were led in song by a country music star, who had been up all night playing dice. A dozen jet bombers flew over. Sixty majorettes thrust out their chests.

This time the man rose with everyone else, and he sang. He sang as loud as he could, in an ear-splitting voice that could be heard twenty rows in any direction.

A few people turned and looked at him as if he were odd.

When the song reached the "land of the free" his voice cracked, but he shrieked out the high note.

Then it was over, everyone applauded, yelled "Kill 'em," and "Murder 'em," and "Belt 'em," and sat down to await the opening kickoff.

Everyone but the one man. He remained on his feet and began slowly singing the second stanza in his loud voice.

People stared at him. But then they jumped up and cheered as the ball was kicked off and run back.

When they sat down, the man was still standing, singing.

He paused for a moment, took a deep breath, and started the third stanza.

"Hey, that's enough," someone yelled.

"Yeah, sit down. I can't see through you," said somebody else.

He kept singing. People called out:

"Knock it off."

"What's wrong with him?"

"I can't see."

The game was under way. Three plays were run while he sang the third verse.

Everyone jumped up for the punt return. When they sat down, the man was still singing.

Everyone around him was becoming upset. People

stood and shook their fists. Somebody threw a hot-dog wrapper.

An usher asked him to take his seat. He shook his head and began the fourth stanza as a touchdown was scored.

The people behind him were outraged. "I couldn't see that because of you . . . Make him sit down . . . He must be crazy . . . He's a radical . . ."

He went on singing.

Somebody grabbed his shoulders and tried to push him into his seat. They scuffled and swung their programs. Somebody dropped a hip flask. The man struggled to his feet, still howling the fourth stanza.

A policeman pushed through. "What's going on? Break it up."

"He won't sit down," someone yelled. "He won't stop singing," someone else said. "He's trying to start a riot. He's a radical."

"Let's go, fella," the policeman said, leading him away as he finished the final stanza, holding the note as long as he could.

The judge fined him $25 for disorderly conduct, and warned him about not shouting fire in a crowded theater.

The next week he went to the Amazing Bowl. The crowd was led in singing the National Anthem by a rock star, who had been up all night with three groupies. A squadron of dive bombers flew between the goal posts.

He stood with everyone else. As the music was played, he moved his lips because he was chewing peanuts, and he stared at the chest of a majorette. Then he sat down with everyone else.

The man in the next seat offered him a sip from his flask.

WOMEN'S LIB GOING BERSERK

January 4, 1972

There are men who laughed at Women's Lib. They thought it was a joke about bras.

Some of them are still laughing. But if they are wise, they will stop laughing and start ducking. The revolution is occurring.

Proof of that has been popping up in little and big stories during the last few days.

Two of the more significant could be found in Chicago's divorce courts.

One was the last divorce of 1971. The other was the first divorce suit filed in 1972.

In the last 1971 divorce, the grounds were physical cruelty. One mate beat the other.

That, in itself, isn't unusual. There have always been men who beat their wives. Such men are beneath contempt. A decent husband can assert his will with a few terrifying threats.

But what was unusual was that the last divorce was sought by a man. He said his wife "beat him about the head and shoulders." And he said she did it often. The judge gave the bruised fellow his freedom.

In the first divorce suit of 1972, the grounds were desertion.

Once again, this isn't unusual. Some men are footloose. They go off to become beachcombers or great painters.

But in this case, the wrong party was the man. He said his wife of seven years packed up and walked out on him, the kid, and their suburban ranch house.

So what? you ask. What do a couple of obscure divorce cases mean?

Coming back-to-back as they did, while the calendar was changing, is an omen.

It is also a warning to men that Women's Lib may not be as delightful a revolution as they had hoped.

Many men thought it merely meant scantier clothes, unfettered chests, and women buying their own drinks.

They thought it meant women no longer considered marriage to be the logical step after holding hands. This pleased men of past generations who were forever choosing between youthful frustration or a quickie marriage in a place like Crown Point, Ind.

But nobody expected wives to beat their husbands about the head and shoulders, or abandon them in their ranch homes.

For those who doubt the significance of the divorce cases, here is further evidence.

Consider which women are admired most by other women, according to the polls.

At the end of 1970, the most admired woman in the United States was Mamie Eisenhower.

Mamie was the classic American female success story: wife, mother, and quiet helpmate, standing in the shadows of a successful man. The grand tradition.

But in the year-end poll of 1971, the most admired woman was Golda Meir.

Mrs. Meir had been around a long time. So why the sudden popularity?

I'll tell you why. All year she has been buying bombs and jet fighters, scaring her enemies, and being recalcitrant.

The same poll shows that Indira Gandhi, who was eighth in 1970, climbed to fourth in 1971.

She led her country to war and she won. Women liked that.

Now it is the hawks, rather than the old hens, who are the heroines.

(It should be noted, however, that Tricia Nixon finished a strong second both years. She probably gets a big sympathy vote.)

Further evidence of change was the chortling I have heard from many women as they read about Moshe Dayan, the dashing eye-patch hero of Israel.

Not long ago, it came out that Dayan's marriage was breaking up. Everybody assumed that Dayan, a romantic sort, had found a younger woman and was leaving his middle-aged wife.

But it turned out that plump Mrs. Dayan found somebody she liked better and is leaving Moshe.

When this can happen to one of the world's most glamorous men, are any of us secure?

This is the inevitable result of revolution. In the beginning, the leaders have solid reforms in mind.

So it was with Women's Lib. The original ideas—women having a fair chance of good jobs, so they could share in the ulcers and shorter life spans; paying alimony; whistling at men; opening their own doors and smoking Cigarillos, and parting without tears as good friends—were fine aspirations.

But in almost all the revolutions some people go too far.

So we have husband-abandonment, husband-beating, and a lust for war.

Responsible leaders, such as Gloria Steinem and Betty Friedan, should renounce such excesses.

Their movement will not be helped by female chauvinist sows.

THINGS TOUGH, BUT HE CAN'T KICK

January 21, 1972

Jim Johnson, 21, who kicked two cheating vending machines, has been told that if he kicks another one, he will be fired from his job.

This, as far as I know, is the first showdown between a machine-kicker and a machine-backer.

Johnson, who is a clerical worker for the Illinois Central R.R., kicked the machines out of a sense of chivalry.

Two girls in his office had put coins in a candy-bar machine and a sweet-roll machine.

The machines accepted the money, but gave nothing in return.

Johnson was standing nearby and the girls said: "Can you fix this damn machine?"

"What was I going to do?" Johnson said. "These were girls and they couldn't kick too well."

Squaring his shoulders and in a capable manner, Johnson stepped back and gave each of the machines a good one. (He used the bottom-of-the-foot kick, as I have always recommended.)

Both machines promptly gave forth candy and sweet rolls.

The girls looked admiringly at Johnson, especially his foot, and he felt rather proud.

But he didn't know the entire scene had been observed by an informant, a spy, a company fink, or maybe somebody who was jealous of Johnson's success with the ladies.

Whoever the observer was, Johnson was reported to management. A few days later he was called in by his boss.

"When I went in, they had a railroad cop there," Johnson said.

"My boss, Mr. Kelly, asked me if I was in the cafeteria Saturday. Sort of like a police routine.

"I told them, sure, I was in the cafeteria Saturday.

"Then Mr. Kelly said he had received a complaint from an employee who saw what I did. He asked me if I had done it.

"I said, sure, I did it, that I kick machines all the time.

"Actually, that was only the second time I ever kicked a machine. The only other machine I kicked is the dollar-changing machine when it took me for a dollar. That's a lot of money to lose.

"Mr. Kelly got very irate that I thought the whole thing was funny. He said that the machine was broken.

"And the policeman said that he had investigated and found heel marks on the machine.

"They said that they thought I might have broken the

machines by kicking them, because on Monday they didn't work.

"I told them that of course they didn't work on Monday, because they weren't working very good on Saturday. I wouldn't have kicked them if they had been working right. A person doesn't kick a machine when it works. What is the sense of that?

"They said they didn't like my attitude. They didn't like the idea that I would mistreat a machine, even if it cheated people."

That meeting ended with Johnson's case being taken under study.

A couple of days later, Johnson was called in again and the verdict was delivered. He was under a sort of probation.

The terms are that he cannot kick the machine again.

"They said that kicking a machine is a very serious matter and that if I did it again, I could be fired.

"I am allowed to put a dime in, but I cannot do anything to the machine if it steals my money. I told them that I've lost money before and never got it back. They said that in the future they will make sure I am reimbursed."

How about a punch?

"I can't punch them either."

Maybe putting a shoulder to it.

"Nothing. I can't lay a finger on it."

As folk-music fans know, the most famous railroad employe of them all was John Henry, a steel-driving man.

It was John Henry who stood up to a new machine that was brought in to replace him and others. He challenged it to a spike-driving contest.

Legend has it that John Henry drove more steel than the machines (this was before they had unions).

The heroic effort killed John Henry, but his memory lives, especially on 33 rpm records.

Give the candy machine one more kick, Jim Johnson. Don't you want people to sing about you someday?

WOMEN'S LIB: ANOTHER SIDE

A few days ago, two California women turned down alimony because they believe in Women's Lib. They said alimony would prevent them from being truly independent and equal. Their ex-husbands didn't argue.

If this practice ever becomes widespread, it will take all of the excitement out of Barry Levy's job.

Levy is a deputy sheriff and his job is hunting down men who don't believe in alimony and child support.

This is challenging work because many men do not subscribe to alimony.

"Consider John," said Deputy Levy. "What a time he

188

gave us. We go to his mother's house and she says he's not there. So we look around.

"Then we go up to the second floor, a vacant flat.

"I open a cabinet under the kitchen sink. There is John."

Deputy Chuck Givines said: "I had one who was even trickier than that.

"A couple of weeks ago, I went to a guy's girl friend's apartment.

"She told me: 'No, he's not living with me anymore.'

"So I asked her if I could look around. She said, sure, he's not here.

"We got to the bathroom, and there's a big bathtub full of clothes.

"I had a hunch, so I turned on the water in the tub. A minute later, he comes up from under the clothes.

"As I put the cuffs on him, I asked him what he was doing there in the bathtub. He said: 'I was looking for a clean pair of socks.' "

"Then there was a guy," Givines went on, "who we found behind some luggage in his closet. I asked him why he was in his closet. He said he was looking for a shirt.

"But there was one guy I really felt sorry for. He was living with his second wife, but he wasn't making payments to his first wife.

"When we got there, his second wife started yelling: 'He's not here. He's not here.'

"But all the time she's yelling, she's pointing at the bed. We looked under the bed and there he was.

"His wife asked where we were taking him. We told her: 'To jail.' She said, 'Good. Now my boy friend can come over.' "

Which reminded another deputy, Pat Danna, of a story.

"I had this guy who jumped from his second-floor

bedroom window to a nearby roof, then he took off down an alley.

"It was the dead of winter, and all he had on were his shorts.

"When I caught him, I asked him where he thought he was going. He said: 'I knew you were arresting me, so I was going to tell a friend to come and bail me out.' "

Which reminded deputy Joe Seals of a story.

"I got to his girl friend's house and naturally she says he isn't there.

"So I look around and when I go in the bathroom, I looked in the shower. There he is, nude, just like he came into the world.

"I said, 'Let's go.' But he says: 'I know the law. You can't take me in.'

"I said: 'Why can't I?'

"And he says: 'Because you got to see my face to iden-tify me. And all you see is my back.'

"I told him that the law was satisfied if I saw his back."

Deputy Seals went on. "I'll tell you about the trickiest one I ever had.

"I had been after him for a long time, but he was always ahead of me. Then I got word he had a girl friend.

"I went to her place late at night and she was real helpful. She said I could look around all I wanted, that there was nobody there but her and her sister.

"I looked in one of the bedrooms, and there was a woman in bed, sleeping.

" 'That's my sister,' she said.

"I was ready to leave when I got a hunch. I went back in the bedroom and pulled back the covers.

"It was him, and he had on all his clothes. He was wearing one of his girl friend's wigs."

People should give Women's Lib a chance.

ACUTE
CRISIS
IN
IDENTITY

February 18, 1972

The "identity crisis" has become a common ailment in our society. People wonder who they really are. Sometimes they have to go off and find themselves.

This occurs most often among young people. When it happens they sing sad songs about it, or renounce their parents' central air-conditioning, smoke strange things, put flowers in their hair, eat an organically grown peanut, or assume the lotus position.

It happens to adults, too, although not as often.

Grown women seldom have an identity crisis while raising small children. When a woman has diapers to

191

change, she knows who she is: She is the person who changes diapers.

But when the children get older and go to school, she isn't sure anymore. So she might go back to college and study philosophy, great literature, or ceramics. Or she might get involved in Women's Lib, which can make her even more confused.

For a man, it is simpler. His identity crisis might hit him at about 7:45 a.m. while stuck on an expressway with the sun in his left eye. Then he might think: "Why am I here? Why was I here yesterday? Will I be here tomorrow?" In most cases, the man manages to change lanes and he feels better.

But if it becomes acute, he could clean out the joint savings account and go off to find himself maybe in Las Vegas and in the arms of a painted woman.

Until recently, my knowledge of the identity crisis came from reading advice columnists and other scientific journals, and from talking to my 17-year-old nephew, who is a guru and is into a diet of organically grown guitar picks.

As for myself, I never had an identity crisis. I have always known who I am, which, while deeply depressing, saved me a lot of running around looking for me.

But now it has happened to me. I have had my identity crisis. It came about in a strange way.

Hoping to be one of the American journalists accompanying President Nixon to China, I decided to get a passport.

The State Department said I would need a birth certificate to get a passport. It is a rule.

I didn't have one, and did not remember ever seeing it. Few occasions arise in which you must have written proof that you were born.

So I went to the office of County Clerk Edward J. Barrett, where all Chicago births are kept on file. I made out the form and paid the man $2.

In a few minutes, he had gone through the files, found the old document, and handed me a Xeroxed copy.

As I read it, my identity crisis exploded.

Almost everything on the document was correct. The hospital, the date, the parents.

But it said my name was Mitchell.

Not Michael. Not Mike. Not any of the names I have been known by—Goofy, Stop Thief, Hey You, Creep, Obnoxious—but Mitchell.

I went back to the counter and pointed to the name and asked the clerk: "What does this mean?"

He said: "Is this your birth certificate?"

"Yes."

He studied it a moment, then said: "It means your first name is Mitchell."

I said: "But nobody has ever called me Mitchell."

He nodded. "I suppose they called you Mitch."

My head swam. At least it swam faster than it usually swims.

How could my name have been Mitchell all of these years without my knowing it? And if it was Mitchell, why have I always thought it was Michael?

Several ideas came to me. Maybe the real Mitchell Royko had been misplaced by a nurse. And somebody named Michael put in his crib by mistake. You hear about hospitals doing such things. If that had happened, who was I? And where was he?

I pondered this a while, then concluded that it made no sense.

Then it occurred to me that maybe twins had been born—one named Mike and one named Mitch. But I would have noticed him as we grew up. We had a small flat.

Whatever the explanation was, one thing was perfectly clear: I wasn't me. According to the office of Edward J. Barrett, county clerk, I was somebody named Mitchell.

But I could not be Mitchell, since my name is Michael on my Playboy Club key. Yet, there was no record of the birth of Michael, so I wasn't either Michael or Mitchell.

Then, who was I? Maybe Kup?

I began feeling like a teen-ager.

Despite the panic, I saw obvious benefits in having a new name. I could put an ad in the personals: "Responsible for my own debts only and not that other guy's. Mitchell Royko." Then off to Las Vegas.

But that would not clear up the mystery, and ease my identity crisis. So I went to older relatives and asked them if they remembered anything strange about my birth.

"Only you," one of them said.

But there was something. A relative remembered it, and I'm convinced it is the answer.

"The doctor was called to St. Mary's Hospital from a wedding on Milwaukee Ave.," he said. "So he walked funny.

"I think when he slapped you, like they slap newborn babies to make them breathe, he might have slapped you in the head."

That explains many things, but not the name.

"Yes, but afterwards the doctor and your father went over to a place on North Av. to have a couple of drinks."

To celebrate?

"There are other reasons to drink. And after they had a few, the doctor wasn't thinking too clearly, and he didn't know much English anyway, so he probably wrote in the wrong first name."

I'm satisfied that is the explanation, undramatic as it may be.

If the doctor had to make a mistake, though, I wish it had been in the date. A change in one figure, and I could be 19—officially. But then I'd just brood about why a young kid like me has got falling hair.

A
RED
HATER
GETS
A
SHOCK

February 20, 1972

A scientist friend of mine has a Time Machine and we sometimes take trips.

Yesterday, while drifting backwards in time, we decided to buy a few nostalgic phonograph records, so we stopped in the year 1950.

As we stepped from the machine, a young man jumped back and stammered: "What are you, Russian invaders?"

We hurriedly identified ourselves and told him about the Time Machine.

Intrigued, he asked us what things are like in 1972.

"I wouldn't know where to start," I said. "Everything is so different."

"Then tell me about politics," he said. "That's my chosen career."

We sat down and I tried to fill him in.

"To begin with, the President has just returned from a trip to China."

The man clapped his hands. "Wonderful. Then Chiang Kai-shek has finally driven the Communists out. I knew he would do it."

"I'm afraid not. The fact is China is 100 per cent Communist."

He looked puzzled. "Then what was the President doing there?"

"Oh, eating, drinking, seeing the sights, talking to the leaders."

"Drinking?" the man said.

"Sure. He drank a toast to China."

"What in the hell for?"

"As a matter of fact, he even quoted from the Little Red Book of Wise Sayings of Mao Tse-tung in his toast."

The man sat still for a moment, then said: "What else did he do?"

"Oh, there was so much. They had a big banquet and the President went around to most of the Communist leaders and generals and clinked glasses with them."

The man's face was growing pale.

"Let me see. Oh, yes, he went to the Chinese ballet. The plot was how brave Communists overcome the cruel capitalists."

The man cried out: "I hope he walked out on it."

"As a matter of fact, he told Chou En-lai that he had never seen a finer ballet. He liked it as much as the Chinese orchestra."

"Orchestra?"

"Yes. During the banquet, Chinese musicians played some old American tunes, and the President said he had never heard our music played better."

"That's treason," the man cried. "Hasn't he ever heard Guy Lombardo?"

After he calmed down, we resumed.

"There was also a trip to the Great Wall of China. The President liked that. He said it was a great wall."

The man shook his head slowly.

"And his wife had a great time. She especially liked Chou. She said he's a real charmer, has a delightful sense of humor, and is a man who knows the world. The President seemed to like Chou too. Helped him on with his coat once."

The man's eyes began to roll in his head, so we paused to revive him. "Anything else?" he finally gasped.

"If I remember right, the President looked at some pictures of Trotsky and Marx, or maybe it was Lenin."

"I hope," the man said, "that he said what godless monsters they were."

"No, if I remember correctly he said they were 'great philosophers.' "

We wrapped the man in blankets and took the other precautions against shock. Then I went on.

"Naturally, the main purpose of the trip was to sit down and talk things over—you know, the diplomatic give-and-take."

"What did they give us?" he said.

"Two pandas."

He shook his head weakly. "And what did we give them?"

"Two musk oxen and Taiwan."

"Taiwan?" he gasped.

"Possibly. We said we'd take our troops out and sort of said we'd mind our own business."

A large tear ran down the man's nose. He put his face in his hands and said:

"Then everything I've done is wasted. My dedicated service on the House Un-American Activities Committee. My wonderful bill to register Commie front organizations with the government. All wasted. My fearless election campaigns against those who are 'soft on Communism,' my battles against those pinkos who got their training in Dean Acheson's College of Cowardly Communist Containment. That's all wasted.

"Not to even mention my fearless attacks on the Truman-Acheson gang's toleration and defense of Communism in high places. All these fine phrases wasted."

His voice cracked. "My entire career—all aimed at saving our country from internal and external Commies— a waste."

He was so crushed, I had to reassure him. "Believe me," I said, "it isn't a waste."

"But you said . . ."

I stopped him. "It wouldn't be right to tell you everything, but I'll tell you this much: You will be very big on the political scene in 1972."

The color returned to his cheeks. "How big?"

"Real big. In fact, when we left you were considered the heavy favorite in the presidential election."

He sprang to his feet and pumped our hands, while shouting: "Then all is not lost for our nation."

As we climbed back into the Space Machine, he was shouting: "And I'll win. I'll lambaste him as a Com-symp, a pinko, a China collaborator, soft on Communism . . ."

And he had both his arms in the air, making V's with his fingers.

THEY
REIGN
IN
THEIR
PARADE

March 17, 1972

Few days are as festive and joyous for all Chicagoans as St. Patrick's Day.

Although it is an Irish observance, people of all ethnic and racial backgrounds take part because, as Mayor Daley is fond of saying:

"Everybody in Chicago is Irish on St. Patrick's Day."

And to a visitor, that might appear to be true. In City Hall and other government offices, just about everyone wears a touch of green, whether they are Irish or something else.

The Chicago River is dyed green, and green water spurts from the fountain in the Civic Center Plaza.

Regardless of what they usually serve, most restaurants add corned beef and cabbage to their menu, and some put green coloring in the beer.

But the true spirit of the day can be seen at the great parade down State St., with a green stripe painted down the center of the road.

While most marchers in the front of the parade are Irish—including such officials as the mayor, the assessor, the president of the County Board, the county clerk, the police chief, and the fire chief—following behind are many individuals and organizations representing other nationalities, most of them sporting the symbolic shamrock, the Irish walking sticks and green hats.

Naturally, you'll find a few spoilsports who don't take part in some way, and to them the mayor's friends jokingly boast: "There are only two kinds of people—those who are Irish, and those who wish they were Irish."

Of course, this isn't the only such annual observance in Chicago. Another popular event is the feast day of San Juan Bautista, held in June.

Although it is a Puerto Rican observance, people of all ethnic backgrounds take part because, as Mayor Daley is fond of saying:

"On the feast day of San Juan Bautista, everybody in Chicago in Puerto Rican."

And to a visitor, that might appear to be true. In City Hall and other government offices, just about everyone wears the "pava," which is the Puerto Rican straw hat.

Most restaurants add roast pig and boiled green bananas to their menu, and some put festive coloring in the rum.

But the true spirit of the day can be seen at the great Puerto Rican feast-day parade down State St.

While the marchers in front are Puerto Rican, they are followed by those of other groups, including the mayor, the assessor, the president of the County Board, the police chief, and the fire chief, all wearing their "pava" hats and Puerto Rican peasant costumes.

Naturally, you'll find a few spoilsports who won't take part. But to them the mayor's friends jokingly boast: "There are only two kinds of people—those who are Puerto Rican, and those who wish they were Puerto Rican."

Then there is Jan. 15, which is Martin Luther King's birthday.

Although it is primarily a black observance, people of all ethnic and racial backgrounds take part, because as Mayor Daley is fond of saying:

"Everybody in Chicago is an African on Martin Luther King's birthday."

And to a visitor that might appear to be true. In City Hall and other government offices, just about everybody is wearing an African dashiki.

The Chicago River is dyed black, and black water spurts from the fountain in the Civic Center Plaza.

Most restaurants add chitterlings, hog maw, roast 'possum, and black eyed peas to their menus, and some put black coloring in the beer.

But the spirit of the day can be seen in the King Day parade down State St., with the black stripe down the center of the road.

While Jesse Jackson, C. T. Vivian, Tom Todd, and other black leaders march in front, they are followed by such people as the mayor, the president of the County Board, the assessor, the police chief and fire chief, all wearing the traditional African dashiki.

A few non-black spoilsports don't take part in some way, and to them the mayor's friends jokingly boast: "There are only two kinds of people—those who are Africans and those who wish they were Africans."

Another joyous time is Hanukkah. Although it is a Jewish observance, just about everybody else joins in, because as Mayor Daley is fond of saying:

"During Hanukkah, everybody in Chicago is a Jew."

When you think about it, these special days, which every ethnic group has, are one of the reasons the people of Chicago get along so well together.

MIDDLEMAN
AMERICA

A new villain has emerged in our society: the Middleman.

He's the person being blamed by almost everybody for the sudden leap in the cost of eating.

Farmers say they aren't making the profit. The food stores say the same thing.

It's the Middleman who is lining his pockets, messing up Phase II and causing housewives to wring their hands at the soaring costs of the flesh of dead animals.

It is strange, but after having eaten about 40,000 meals in my lifetime (not counting snacks and gum I swallowed), I have not once given thought to the existence of a Middleman being involved in my meal. I just wolf it down.

But after listening to all of the experts talk, I decided to track down the Middleman and expose him.

He is harder to locate than you might think, despite his sudden notoriety.

My search began on LaSalle St., with that strange breed of brokers who make a career of gambling on what a carload of grits or a batch of pork bellies will be worth next month.

I figured that if anyone is a Middleman, it's a man in a $200 suit who buys and sells pork bellies without eating any.

But the brokers deny that they are Middlemen, or have anything to do with the cost of food.

"The commodity brokers are not Middlemen," said broker Michael Maduff. "Joseph in the Bible was the first commodity broker."

That was news to me.

"Yes, he believed that there was going to be a shortage seven years hence. He stored up grain and then seven years hence, when there was a food shortage, he sold food to consumers and kept people from starving."

Broker Maduff said the blame for the rise in food prices rests with the consumer.

That would include a lot of people, since just about everybody eats food, except those young people who eat flowers.

"Consumers want meat," Maduff said, "and they are the ones who drive the prices up."

I hadn't thought about it that way. It's the old law of supply and demand. If we would all stop eating food, they'd have to come down in price. Well, it's an idea.

But another broker disagreed. Roy Pavich says: "Either the supermarkets are doing it or the meat packers."

Then they must be the notorious Middlemen?

"That's pretty hard to say," said Pavich. "He (the Middleman) is pretty sheltered."

Still another broker blamed the fiscal policies of the government.

"Balance the budget," said Frederick Uhlmann. "As long as you spend more money than you take in, that's inflationary."

Sound advice, but that didn't get me any closer to the elusive Middleman.

So I turned to the Agriculture Department in Washington, which has been one of the leading accusers of the Middleman.

I phoned, got an official on the line, and told him I wanted to know who the Middleman is.

"Who?" he said.

"The Middleman."

"I'm not sure I understand."

"You know, the one who is making the fast profit on the food."

"I see," he said, becoming silent for several moments. "Let me transfer you."

Another official came on, listened, then said:

"Well, you'll have a hard time pinning him (the Middleman) down. You see, there are so many of them."

Just give me a few, so I can expose them and we can all smoke a good five-cent steak again.

Middlemen, he said, include the truck driver who hauls the doomed beast from the farm, and his employer. Or the railroad or barge, if they are shipped that way.

And the man who whacks the cow on the head, and the man who pays him to. And the guy in the bloody apron with the long knife, and his employers.

If it's to be frozen, the freezing people are Middlemen, and so are the cellophane makers, who give you a peek at only the lean side of the chop.

Warehouses, where food sits awaiting our molars, are

Middlemen, and so are the additive makers who inject the chemicals that let it wait in the warehouses without turning mossy.

"Take a can of chicken soup," said the Agriculture official. "The chicken must be transported, and processed before it gets into the can. So do the vegetables. Then there is the can itself, and paper for the label, and the printing for the label. And the cartons in which they are packed, and the people who ship them. All of these are Middlemen. You can't count the number of Middlemen who are involved in a can of soup."

I may never eat again, now that I know how many people have their hands in my mouth.

CAPT. INGHAM GETS HIS MAN

Lonny Murphy, sole owner of the Sweet Daddy Fruit and Vegetable Co., starts his work day at dawn.

His wife and kids are still sleeping when he slips into his baggy jeans and drives his truck from their West Side flat to the South Water market.

By 8:30 a.m., he has bought his produce, driven to an empty lot on 4110 W. Madison, and is unloading the truck.

By 9 a.m. his outdoor stand is set up, the fruit and vegetables are on display, the scale is hooked to the back of his truck, his helper has arrived, and he is open for business.

"This is it," says Lonny, a tall, husky man of 38, waving his arm at the 12-foot-long vegetable stand.

"That's the Sweet Daddy Fruit and Vegetable Co. You see it all. It ain't the A&P, but I take care of my family.

He's usually there until about 6 p.m.—later when the days get longer. And he takes only Sundays off, so we're talking about a 72-hour week.

Years ago he did common labor. Then he drove a cab. Later he bought an old truck and did general hauling.

About a year ago, he set up his fruit and vegetable stand. It's not a bad location because there isn't a food store within four blocks in any direction. In that part of black Lawndale, Madison St. is loaded with clothing stores, furniture stores, TV stores, and other high-profit, time-payment businesses.

But not many people want to sell groceries.

"In a good week," Lonny says, "I'll make about $150. In a bad week? I've had weeks when the weather was so cold I didn't make expenses. And this week—man, this week gonna be bad."

This week's going to be bad because Lonny has spent most of his time loading his produce back in the truck, instead of selling it.

Monday, for instance, three squad cars arrived just when afternoon trade was picking up.

A sergeant told him: "If you aren't out of here in 15 minutes, I'll run you in."

Lonny showed him his city peddler's license, but the sergeant said: "You heard. Fifteen minutes."

On Tuesday, a foot patrolman came by and told him to move. Lonny moved, but he returned later and set up. He got in an hour of business before a squad ran him off.

That night he went to the Fillmore Station and asked the captain what was going on?

"I told him I been selling there for six months. Nobody bothered me. I sell at fair prices. People appreciate it because it's convenient.

"The men who own the stores on the street, they like me bein' here. Me and my helper keep the punks from bustin' in parked cars. Out here we can see everything.

"Before we opened, punks was snatching purses. But we caught 'em and roughed 'em up a little and now that don't happen.

"So I ask the captain why they botherin' me now?"

"He tell me the heats on. He says there's nothing he can do and the blue coats gonna chase me away."

Lonny shook his head uncomprehendingly.

"What kind of heat he talkin' 'bout? Who am I botherin'? I'm only tryin' to live and make a livin' for amy family. I ain't here to rip off nobody. We just peddling.

"Heats on. I don't understand how cruel a man can be."

While he talked, a shabbily dressed old woman stopped at the stand, ordered two large sweet potatoes, paid with coins from a small change purse, and moved on.

"That woman lives 'round the corner," Lonny said. "She don't have a car, so if I wasn't here, she have to walk 'bout a mile extra to buy some potatoes. That makes me a criminal?"

His head turned sharply. "Oh-oh, here he comes."

Down the street came a foot patrolman. He stopped at the corner, stared at Lonny, took out his pocket two-way, and talked into it.

Before long, a squad car pulled up, a policeman got out and said: "OK, pack it up. Now!"

Lonny picked up a crate of apples, hauled it to the rear of his truck, shoved it in, and softly groaned: "Shee-it!"

At the Fillmore Police Station, the acting commander, Capt. Frederick G. Ingham, tersely said:

"We've got an awful lot of complaints from all the stores over there—Walgreen's, Goldblatt's, the restaurants. He's cutting in on their business. They sell food, too.

"Even if he does have a peddler's license, he's got to keep moving. Any man who is peddling in that area, we've warned. They make it look like Maxwell St."

(When I was there, Lonny's operation didn't look anything at all like Maxwell St. It looked like an outdoor vegetable stand.)

"When I get a complaint," said Capt. Ingham, "I take action. When somebody complains, let's do something about it! I've got a job to do and this is the only way I can do it."

But what about a man who is just trying to make a living and isn't bothering anyone?

"You tear my heart out," said the captain.

And those store keepers who say Lonny keeps away auto thieves and purse snatchers?

"I'll tell you what," said the captain, with poorly concealed sarcasm, "if somebody will document that for us, we will give this gentleman a citizen's award."

What about staying in business?

"No."

Somehow, I can't believe that giants like Walgreen's, Goldblatt's are being threatened by Lonny Murphy eking out his living near them. In fact, I wasn't aware they sold sweet potatoes.

But I do believe that there are men who become officious little tyrants when they put on a uniform and get a couple of bars on their shoulder.

So don't bother pulling at your bootstraps, Lonny.

Go and put in for welfare. Just tell 'em Capt. Ingham sent you.

MA'S QUIET TAX REVOLT

Every April 15, when taxes are due, I think of my mother.

That probably sounds strange because most people think of their mothers at such times as Mother's Day or Christmas.

I do that, too. But also on April 15 because long before anyone mentioned a "tax revolt," my mother waged one.

She did it quietly, and nobody but her children knew about it, but she did it.

For about 20 years, while earning a taxable income running her own small business, she didn't pay a nickel of income tax.

She didn't use loopholes. She wouldn't have under-stood them.

Ma just didn't bother to file a return all those years. She simply ignored the existence of the Internal Revenue Service.

I know that sounds like outright tax evasion, rather than a tax revolt, but the distinction has to do with motive.

If a well-to-do person doesn't pay because he wants two Cadillacs instead of one, that would be evasion.

But if there just isn't enough for both you and the government, that amounts to self-defense.

As my mother explained it:

"I need it more than the government does. Besides, they'd probably waste it anyway."

You couldn't argue with that. During many of those years, she supported her family in her tiny tailor shop, sit-ting at a sewing machine 12 hours a day, six days a week. And that brought in just enough to get by.

If she paid taxes, she would have had to work 14 hours a day. Enough is enough, Congressmen don't work that hard, except when they are weaving new tax loop-holes for the rich.

And none of the money was wasted. It was spent on the ingredients for large pots of soup, oil for the stove in the parlor, and repairs on the old Singer sewing machine. But if the government got it, it would just design another military transport plane that can't fly.

As to the possibility that she would be caught and pros-ecuted, since it was a criminal offense, she said:

"I'll tell them to put me in prison. If they won't let me support myself, then they can support me."

But she wasn't caught, and now it is too late, so I can admit that Ma got away with a pretty good one.

And why not? We are told of millionaires who pay no

income tax, thanks to loopholes created for them by Congress.

J. Paul Getty, one of the world's richest men, is said to pay only $5,000 or so on an annual income of more than $50 million.

If true, Getty pays only one-tenth of one-tenth of one-tenth of one-tenth of his income. My mother would have gladly paid under those terms. It would have amounted to about 30 cents.

The laws are so crafty that if a rich heiress puts $1 million into municipal bonds, she gets back about $50,000 a year—tax free.

But if a scrub lady sweats to save $1,000 and puts it into a savings and loan, she gets back about $50 a year— and has to share the $50 with the federal government.

The loopholes are for the rich. For the ordinary person, the loophole turns into a noose.

Despite this, we hear Treasury Sec. John Connally saying of tax reform: "It leaves me cold." Then he launches a widely publicized crackdown on the storefront tax preparers. You bet, because they are cheating for the hand-to-mouth crowd. But there's no crackdown on millionaires.

We hear the Vice-President carp about a welfare mother chiseling an extra dollar or two, but he doesn't say a word about the big real estate write-offs, oil depletion, and those who pay only one-tenth of one-tenth of one-tenth of one-tenth.

If the tax laws are reformed, it will amount to merely throwing a few crumbs in the direction of the ordinary worker. The cake will remain right where it is.

What this country needs, for genuine reform, are a few million people who had my mother's attitude.

It is a foolish dream, of course, but let us imagine for a

moment that a few million hard-pressed people said: "Sorry, there's not enough for both of us, so put me in jail."

The computers would catch them. But where would they find enough judges and prosecutors to try them?

And where would they find a jury of their peers to convict them? You would need a jury composed of J. Paul Gettys to find guilty a man who said:

"Sure, I didn't pay taxes. I have to work two jobs to barely support my family. Go get it from H. L. Hunt."

If that happened on a big scale, we would have tax reform, and we'd have it faster than you can say IT&T.

But it won't happen, because few of us have enough courage. I got my check in on time, and I probably paid more than old man Getty. Ma would be ashamed of me.

CABDRIVER'S GRAND COUP

The people from the various night shifts who drink in Billy Goat's Tavern are still talking about the wonderful thing that happened to the cabdriver.

They say it began a little after midnight last Thursday. The place was half-filled, but quiet. Most heads faced the TV or their beer glasses.

Then the door opened and laughter and chatter drifted in, followed by six or seven happy people.

They were well dressed and sounded as if Billy Goat's wasn't their first stop of the evening, especially a woman who had a bottle of Greek brandy in her hand.

They lined up at the bar and one of them slapped

down a $20 bill. "Give everybody in the house a drink," he said.

That woke the place up. A printer pushed his beer stein away and switched to double Jack Daniels.

One of the men leaned across the bar and told owner Sam Sianis that he had a very important customer.

Sianis nodded vigorously. Anybody who buys a round for the house is important. The tavern on Hubbard St. is under Michigan Av., but it's more or less a workingman's bar.

The man pointed to one of his companions and identified him as a United States senator from one of the Southern states. He was in town on business, they had been out to dinner in Greek Town, and had stopped in Billy Goat's for a nightcap.

After a round of drinks, the senator said: "We'll need a cab soon, won't we?"

"Will you call a cab?" one of the men asked the bartender.

The bartender phoned and said a U.S. senator in Billy Goat's needed a cab.

A few minutes later, the door opened, and a white-haired man in horned-rim glasses, about 50, came in and said: "Who called for a cab?"

The senator's party greeted him like an old friend. By 1 a.m., people often act as if everybody is an old friend.

"Have a drink," one of them said to the cabby.

The cabby looked them over, nodded, and hauled himself onto a stool.

"What'll you have?" the bartender asked.

Just then the senator asked for a bourbon and water.

"Make it two," the cabby said.

He finished that drink and glanced at the clock.

"Don't worry about time," one of the men said, stuffing a few bills into the cabby's shirt pocket. "Have another drink."

"Don't mind if I do," said the cabby.

He finished that one, didn't look at the clock, and started chatting with his new companions. Every few minutes one of them would stuff a bill into his shirt or jacket pocket.

By 1:30 a.m., they were talking about Chicago politics, and somebody mentioned Vito Marzullo, a West Side ward boss.

"Vito's my buddy," yelled the cabby, and launched into a speech about Vito's greatness. Somebody stuffed another bill in his shirt pocket.

The woman with the Greek brandy bottle told him to try a glass.

"I'll try anything," grinned the cabdriver. The woman poured him a glass and dropped the bottle.

Somebody mentioned something important to the senator, who decided to jot it down.

"Give me a pencil and paper," the senator said to the bartender.

"Make that two," yelled the cabby.

"Two what?" the bartender said.

Finally, as closing time neared, someone said: "We'd better get going."

The cabdriver carefully got off the stool and stood up. He gazed across the bar at Sianis and slowly said:

"Bartender, call us a cab. We're leaving."

Sianis said: "You're the cabdriver. We called you."

The cabby nodded, turned and slowly led the way out onto Hubbard St.

He opened a door of his cab and got into the back seat.

"Let's go," he yelled.

Shouting and laughing, everybody piled in, the cab pulled away from the curb and disappeared into the night.

"I couldn't tell who was driving," Sianis said later. "Maybe it was the senator."

PENNY-ANTE
BYSTANDERS

Life in the big, wunnerful city.

It was a warm night. Rena Friedman and her boy friend, Bob Donofrio, walked down to the Oak St. beach.

People were throwing Frisbees, strumming guitars, sitting around, strolling.

Rena and Bob dangled their feet in the water, watched the reflection of the moon and talked.

They sat a long time. When they looked around, they saw that everyone else had drifted away.

Everybody except two men who walked very slowly, veering slightly toward the couple.

Donofrio tensed, he had a hunch that the two men weren't out looking at the stars. Having been mugged four times in his 26 years, Donofrio has learned to trust his hunches.

Miss Friedman got nervous, too. She's never been mugged, but once she was hit on the head with a baseball bat by a would-be rapist. Fortunately, a car with a noisy muffler frightened the batsman away.

So, out of the corners of their eyes, they watched the two men.

Their instincts were correct. The men stopped, one of them grabbed Donofrio's arm, and said: "You got money?"

The other glared at Miss Friedman and said: "Gimme your jewelry."

While Miss Friedman took off her wristwatch, and placed it on the ground, Donofrio stood up.

Suddenly, to give his girl a chance to run, he pulled his arm away, stepped back a few feet, and began calling the men obscene names.

They turned on him, and Miss Friedman started running toward the Outer Drive.

"Get her," one of the men yelled.

Miss Friedman, 24, runs well and screams loud. When she got to the drive she darted into traffic, causing several cars to slam on their brakes and prompting her pursuer to turn around.

Meanwhile, Donofrio, who grew up in a tough neighborhood, was doing quite well. In fact, the two men weren't getting much more than a draw out of the brawl.

And Miss Friedman's screams caused several cars to stop. People got out to see that was happening, and their presence made the muggers back off.

But Miss Friedman didn't know that. For all she knew, her boy friend was being killed.

When she got through traffic, she saw two men looking at her from inside the lobby at 1212 N. Lake Shore, a very prestigious high-rise building. The doorman and another building employe. They had apparently seen her running.

She rushed into the lobby and they stared at her. She was sobbing, her mascara running down her face, and she cried:

"Call the police. Somebody may be getting killed across the street."

The doorman looked at her for a moment. Then he said:

"Do you have a dime?"

I will pause here to let you think about that.

Consider some of the things a person could say when a sobbing, hysterical woman appears and shouts that somebody might be murdered, please call the police.

One might say: "Oh, that's awful." Or: "Holy smoke." Or: "What's that police number again?" Or: "Don't worry, we'll get help." Or: "I hope we're not too late." Or: "Okay, sit tight, help is on the way."

But—do you have a dime?

I doubt if today's young film-makers, who enjoy creating slightly mad, nightmarish scenes, could have come up with a more bizarre response.

Had Miss Friedman not been so hysterical, she might have been caught up in the spirit of the moment, and responded: "No, I gave at the office."

Instead, she screamed: "For God's sake, no. Somebody may be getting killed, call the police."

The two of them looked at each other, mumbled, and slowly began reaching into their pockets.

Miss Friedman feared that they might flip coins to see which one had to spend the dime, so she rushed back outside to look for help.

That's when an unmarked detective car stopped, the

two muggers fled, and Miss Friedman rejoined Donofrio, who was bruised, but not seriously hurt.

The detectives gave the couple a lift. As they drove past the high-rise, the doorman and the other employe were standing outside, craning their necks, and looking from side to side, as if trying to see where the action was.

Or maybe they were looking for somebody who had change for a quarter.

ALINSKY NOT IN THEIR LEAGUE

June 16, 1972

The City Council paid a great tribute to the late Saul Alinsky a few days ago. It refused to name a city park after him.

An independent alderman had suggested that one of the many unnamed little parks in Chicago be called Alinsky Park and equipped with a soapbox because of Alinsky's devotion to free speech.

The other aldermen, who also believe in free speech, except when the mayor tells them to shut up, didn't like the idea.

Alinsky would have been pleased. Their reaction meant they are still aching from the many kicks he gave them. It meant they remember who formed the toughest,

222

most effective community organizations in Chicago. Alinsky's most recent creation—the Citizens Action Program (CAP)—gave Assessor Parky Cullerton heartburn, and now it is leading the fight against the Crosstown Expressway.

The aldermen's reaction got me to wondering who our many parks and playgrounds are named after, besides Presidents such as Lincoln, Grant, Washington, and Jackson.

Once you get past the world-famous names, the locally prominent Indians, and some of the city's early settlers and businessmen, you find that our politicians are fond of honoring the people they like best—themselves.

On the near West Side, for instance, you have the Sain Playground and the Touhy Playground.

For years, Ald. Harry Sain and County Comr. John Touhy ran the 27th Ward, and they ran it well. On election day they made sure that every bum on W. Madison St. voted, at least once.

They also prospered as insurance men. Businessmen in the ward were eager to place their insurance with the Touhy and Sain Agency. If they didn't, they might need insurance.

Then there is Connors Park, on the Near North Side, named after the later State Sen. William (Botchy) Connors.

One of Connors' admirers said of him: "Botchy was the kind of guy who would give you the shirt off his back. Of course, then he'd take the suit, pants, and shoes off you."

On the South Side, there is the Meyering Playground, named after a former alderman and sheriff, William Meyering.

Meyering was the guardian of Cook County's law and order in the days when Al Capone was our most famous citizen.

Roger Touhy, the gangster, once provided this thumbnail description of Sheriff Meyering, while testifying in federal court.

"A fixer," Touhy said.

The South Side also has a Micek Playground, named after the late Frankie Micek, who was a ward sanitation-office superintendent for 21 years, before rising to alderman.

When he passed away, Ald. Micek was eulogized by Mayor Daley as having been a "dedicated and devoted servant of the people." Later, one of his fellow aldermen added the lofty praise: "Frankie always did what he was told."

McGuane Park, in the Mayor's neighborhood, is named after Mr. Daley's old friend and political crony, John McGuane.

McGuane was a park commissioner and, for a brief time, he was the assessor. He never got in trouble as assessor, and he was replaced by Parky Cullerton, who wasn't as lucky.

On the West Side, we have the Horan Playground, named after the late Al Horan, a noted politician.

Mr. Horan was boss of all the Municipal Court bailiffs, and he was known for never having hired anyone who had committed an infamous deed, such as failing to deliver a precinct or being a Republican.

There is a Pietrowski Playground, on the far South Side, named after County Comr. Lillian (Shoutin' Lil) Pietrowski. Miss Pietrowski is known for her shouting.

Then we have Gately Park and Gately Stadium on the far South Side. These were named after a former president of the Park Board. Park commissioners like to name parks after themselves.

Although James Gately was in charge of the parks, he had a fondness for concrete, as do many Chicago political figures. And he once made the remarkable observation that:

"You can have too much grass."

To which the city's high-rise dwellers, parking-lot operators, and bit contractors said: "Amen." After all, grass isn't the only thing that's green.

DENT
LEADS
TO
A
WIPE-OUT

The stoop-shouldered man and his wife came out of the restaurant and walked to their car in the parking lot. He unlocked her door, went around to get in on his side, stopped, and stared at his car.

In the door was a dent. It wasn't a big dent, but it was enough so he saw it immediately.

"Goddamn it," he hissed.

His car was new. It was in the $4,500-to-$5,000 bracket. The paint glowed with Blue Coral wax.

He shook his head and muttered. His wife finally leaned across the seat and asked what was wrong.

"Come on and look," he said.

She got out and shook her head.

226

"This jerk did it," he said, pointing to the big, black car next to his.

"How do you know?" she said.

"This spot was empty when we got here. He's got to be inside eating. This goof did it all right."

To demonstrate, he used his arm to duplicate the way the other car's door would have swung open.

"See?" he said. "If he opened the door hard, and didn't pay any attention, it would hit right . . . HERE!" He swung his arm so his hand touched the dent.

He stood with his hands on his hips, a Bogart-like grimace on his face, staring at the dent. In his eyes, it got bigger and deeper. He could almost see the rust spreading.

"Damn it," he said, running his hand over the dent, the only imperfection in the sleek metal.

The car meant something to him, silly as that can be. It was the only new car he had ever liked, and one of the few he had ever owned. Not only was it new, but it was an imported, foreign job, known for its road-racing handling, classic lines, craftsmanship, glamour.

It was the kind of car he had wanted as a young man, but couldn't afford. Now it was a balding man's toy. But it had a dent in it.

If the dent had come while roaring around an Alpine hairpin turn, pursued by enemy agents in black fedoras, that would have been a different matter. But that couldn't happen, because most of his driving was done on the Kennedy Expressway, dreaming of mountain roads and spies.

Not that it was an expensive dent. For $35 or $40, most body shops would take care of it. But that meant taking it in, leaving it for a day or two. And $35 is $35. Just because an idiot couldn't open his door with care.

That's one of the curses of modern, big city, parking-lot life. Careless strangers can $40 you to death with dents.

Two kinds of people use parking lots. One kind will get in or out of a tight space inch by inch, cranking the wheel, carefully angling the car to avoid making contact. They open the door with care, squeeze their bodies in or out—anything to avoid crunching the next guy's door.

Then there are those who lurch forward, backward, banging, bumping. They fling open the door, sending chips of paint flying, leaving behind one after another of $40 dents.

A person can baby his car, drive like a Wisconsin farmer, vow to get ten years out of his new wheels. But it's a matter of time until he walks out of the place he works, or a restaurant or a shopping center, and finds a $40 crease in the tin. And someday, when he trades it in, the salesman will look at that one dent and say: "A real dog you got here."

The man in the restaurant parking lot thought about those things, then exhaled with resignation, and started to get in his car.

But then he got back out and looked around the lot. Nobody was in sight.

Smiling wickedly, he leaned over and grabbed the windshield wiper on the other car. He gave it a yank. With a loud crack, the whole thing broke off.

Then he went to the other side and tore off the other wiper.

He fumbled through his pockets and found a piece of paper, on which he wrote: "Next time, you SOB, be careful whose car you dent." He put the note on the windshield, and weighed it down with the broken wipers.

Then he got back in his car, carefully backed out of his parking space, and drove away, feeling a little better.

It's a true story. Don't ask me how I know.

RUSH ST.
HAS
A
MIAMI
FAN

July 17, 1972

MIAMI BEACH—After a while a person had to take a break and get away from the sounds of the convention, if only for a few hours, away from the demands of the young, the poor, the minorities, away from the social issues, the cries for reform.

So a few of us decided to spend an afternoon hiding in the quietest place available—out on the ocean.

That's easy to do here. All along the coast are deep-sea fishing boats, available for trips of a few hours or a few days. They all seem to be owned by men named Cap'n Jimmy, Cap'n Johnny, Cap'n Billy, or Cap'n Jack. Surprisingly, Miami Beach doesn't have even one Cap'n Irving or a Cap'n Sol.

We selected Cap'n Jimmy because his boat was clean and he looked sober. Also, he is originally from Quincy, Ill., a town he said "was pretty danged lively for its size. My momma didn't know my daddy drank until one day he came home sober."

We hopped aboard and before long the hooks were baited and in the water, and we were heading due east in the sun and the breeze. The Miami skyline began fading, and with it, the angry, noisy disputes. Out here was only the quiet throb of the engine.

Then Cap'n Jimmy's helper spoke.

"Where ya' from?" he asked.

He was a muscular, black-haired man, bare from the waist up and deeply tanned. He wore wrap-around sunglasses, white deck pants, no shoes.

His job was to keep bait on the hooks, beer in the hand, and to prevent any of us from being pulled overboard by a fish. But most of the time, he just stood around the deck, gazing out to sea, looking healthy, the envy of smog-filled City Man.

"Chicago," one of us answered.

"Ah, Chicago," he said. "I lived in Chicago for 18 years. I was a bartender on Rush St."

Gave it up to lead the good life, right? one of us said. Said to hell with it, and took to the life of the open sea, right? City Man's dream.

"To do this?" he said. "Nah. Listen. I liked tending bar on Rush St. In those days it had class. People who came down there wore shirts and ties.

"The people who worked on Rush St. were like a big family. Everybody knew everybody else. When we'd close at 4 a.m., I'd go over to this restaurant, and everybody would be there—the bartenders, the waitresses, the pimps, the hookers. I'd have breakfast and maybe get me one of the broads. It was like one big happy family."

A happy family life is the backbone of our nation, I said.

"I left there because people started getting crummy. You weren't getting the high-class people any more and I didn't want to take their guff."

So you came here, and turned your back on the land, turning to the simple, uncomplicated life.

"No, I bought a motel. It was in Zion, you know where that is? Good location, a good investment.

"But I'm there only two months, and what happens? One of those big outfits comes in and builds right across from me. They come in with their color TV in every room, the bar, the restaurant, and that took care of me. It cost me $12,000.

"Is that right, for a big outfit to come in and knock me out, just like that, a little businessman? There should be a law against that, right?"

Right. When do the fish start biting?

"They'll bite. So that's when I got out of the motel and came to Florida."

And you've been happy since, clean air, balmy breezes.

"Nah, I still had some money left, so I decided to go into the bar business.

"I found this place in a town north of here. All it had was a carry-out license, but the owner was too old to run a bar. But it was a great location, and all I needed was the bar license.

"After I bought it, I applied for the license, I filled out all the forms. I got my record from Chicago to show I wasn't a criminal.

"Then you know what they did? Yeah, the town turned me down.

"There was this church two blocks away and they said they didn't want no bar near them.

"It wasn't even a regular church. It was one of them off-brand churches. I never even seen them have a mass or nothing.

"Is that right, an off-brand church keeping a guy from earning a living? Do I tell them how to pray?

"So I had to dump that joint, too, and at a big loss, and that's how come I'm down here working on this boat. I'll tell you, it's not an easy life for a guy."

They weren't biting, so we headed in. As we stepped ashore, it felt good to be back on land, away from the sea and all the talk of business monopolies, social injustice, religious intolerance, and the separation of church and state.

THE
MOUSE
THAT
TICKED

As a child I was deprived. I never had a Mickey Mouse wrist-watch.

It wasn't that my parents didn't want to buy one. But in our neighborhood nobody bought watches from a store.

Everybody got their watches from Stanley's tavern. That's because when somebody needed a few dollars or ran up a bar bill they couldn't pay, they went to Stanley with a watch. So Stanley wound up owning a lot of watches, and when someone needed one they bought from Stanley.

When I graduated from grammar school, instead of Mickey Mouse I got a big, round railroad watch bearing the engraved inscription: "To Bruno, with love, Sarah."

Fortunately, not having a Mickey Mouse watch didn't bother me. The only time I even thought of it was when someone asked what time it was. Then I'd throw a tantrum and lie on the floor crying and kicking my feet. After a while, none of the other men in the barracks would ask me the time.

The old desire for a Mickey Mouse watch came back last week. While shopping for a watch in the budget basement of a State Street department store, I saw in a corner of the display case, a genuine, Ingersoll Mickey Mouse.

I didn't even know they made them anymore. Today's parents, I assumed, bought their children Swiss jobs that tell the time, year, date, and play rock 'n' roll chimes.

When the saleswoman asked, "Can I help you?" I thought, why not?

"Yes, I'd like that one there."

"Oh, the Mickey Mouse. Do you want it gift-wrapped?"

"No. Just wind it and I'll wear it."

She froze with her hand in the case. "You'll wear it?"

"Yes."

I could tell she expected an explanation, something about a joke. She was waiting for me to say something so she could laugh. But I said nothing and looked dignified. She shrugged, I paid her, strapped it on, and left.

The strap was the only flaw. It was wide, red, plastic. That's OK for a kid, but a grown man shouldn't have that on his Mickey Mouse watch.

I went to Watts Jewelers, 176 N. State, and asked the short, round man if he had cheap bands.

"Sure. One dollar. I wear them myself. Give me your watch and I'll put it on."

I slipped the Mickey off the red band and handed it to him.

He stood for several seconds just staring at it in the

palm of his hand. Finally he looked up and said, slowly and firmly:

"This is a Mickey Mouse watch."

"Yes, it is."

"You wear it?"

"Of course."

He looked stern and suspicious. "I never seen a man wear a Mickey Mouse watch before."

"Oh, I wear them all the time. Never wear anything but a Mickey Mouse."

He stared at the watch some more. Then he shook his head and repeated: "I never seen a man wear a Mickey Mouse watch before."

It appeared he wouldn't put a band on or return it unless he got an explanation, so I said:

"I never had one when I was a boy."

He brightened. "Oh, in that case, you're entitled." And he cheerfully sold me a black band.

That is the way it has been for several days. Wearing a Mickey Mouse is more fun for an adult than for a child.

There was the bartender who blinked and asked the standard question: "Is that a Mickey Mouse watch?"

"Of course not. Who ever heard of a grown man wearing a Mickey Mouse watch?"

He nodded. Then he looked closer and said: "What ya givin' me? That IS a Mickey Mouse watch." He called out to his wife in back: "Hey c'mere. He's got on a Mickey Mouse watch."

She smiled, a bit confused, and said: "Well, isn't that wonderful?"

And the bank cashier who said: "You really wear that? All the time?"

"Sure. A man's got a right to wear a Mickey Mouse on his wrist, hasn't he?"

"Sure, sure," he said. As I walked away, he added: "Atta boy, atta boy."

This proves it is never too late.

Now, if I can just find a pair of "high tops"—those great boots with the little pocket on the side for a little knife. BOY!

IT'S THE YEAR OF THE JOGGER

For exercise nuts, this is going to be the summer of the jogger.

The jogger is somebody who goes out and runs. That's all there is to it. Some do it because they hope to keep their hearts pumping long enough to see if the world can get even worse. Others are chasing the physical-fitness miracle that will make them look like Paul Newman with his shirt off.

They already are part of the city landscape, running in the parks, along the boulevards, to the commuter stations.

Some of them have even formed jogging clubs, figuring that if they jog as a group they are less likely to be jumped by teen-agers and have their P.F. Fliers stolen.

Men who used to talk about how much they drank over the weekend now get on the elevators and exchange their best time for the mile and swap stories about pains in their sides.

But it won't last. Just as suddenly as it has wheezed onto the exercise scene in the spring, it will limp away in the fall. By midwinter, all that fatty stuff will be clogging up their valves again.

One reason it won't last is that it's unnatural for people to run around city streets unless they are thieves or victims. It makes people nervous to see someone running. I know that when I see somebody running on my street, my instincts tell me to let the dog out after him.

Slats Grobnik summed up the city attitude when he said: "A guy who runs for anything except a bus can't pass a lie box text."

Running through a park in daylight is acceptable, but most people can't get to a park during the day, unless they are aldermen or some other kind of welfare recipient.

A young man with this problem gave up jogging a few days ago because of an unfortunate, but understandable, incident.

He was jogging on a dark street. A woman turned and saw him approaching. His face was flushed, his mouth was gaping, his breathing was heavy.

Naturally, she assumed he had romance on his mind so she started screaming. He got away before the cops could seize him as a fiend. He has vowed never again to move faster than at a shuffle.

But there are other, deeper reasons why jogging can't last.

No exercise can be truly popular in the United States

unless it has two ingredients. First, it must be played with a ball. Second, it must lack any practical application. It can't even be a descendant of something practical. It must be strictly a game.

It is the nature of man to play with a ball, to roll it, bounce it, kick it, hit it, throw it, catch it, chase it, spit on it, knuckle it. Nothing makes us happier.

We begin with stones, snowballs, marbles, and move on to basketballs, baseballs, softballs, volleyballs, footballs, soccer balls, golf balls, tennis balls, bowling balls, Ping-Pong balls, hand balls, squash balls, pool balls, polo balls, croquet balls.

I suspect it goes back to a day when some hairy guy came out of his cave and saw somebody walking below. Just for the fun of it, he dropped a round rock, while shouting "Aannngggg." This has evolved into "Your serve!" and "Play ball."

Since then, when we really want to have fun, we do something with a ball.

Somebody is asking: What about all the other games and sports that don't require a ball?

Yes, there are many such sports and some are popular. But they are not the games that make the nation feverish. That's because most nonball games are practical, either in themselves or in the act from which they descended.

Skiing, track, mountain climbing, and swimming are just ways of getting from one place to another. They have their followers, but how many of us get as excited about a Swede sliding down a mountain on boards, which is as practical a way as any to get to the bottom, as we do when some seven-footer drops a ball through a hoop, which is about as useless an act as I can think of?

Fencing, archery, shooting, boxing, karate, and wrestling are playful forms of homicide. Except for boxing, none has had the lasting popularity of chasing a fly ball.

Yet, what good would it be to be able to chase a fly ball well if you were stuck on a desert island and food was running low. But if you knew how to wrestle, you could twist the neck of the guy who knows how to chase a fly ball, and eat his food.

Fishing can't be included in the discussion because a game that can be played by an 80-year-old woman with a worm isn't really a game. Yet, being able to fish well makes more sense than being able to punt well. But you don't see the world's greatest smelt-catcher on "Wide World of Sports."

So unless they find a way to get a ball in jogging, it won't survive.

Maybe just bouncing a ball as you jog will do it. The sight of a grown man running down a dark street at night, bouncing a basketball, will strike most people as being normal. And if you yell "Fore," people might even ask for an autograph.

MUNICH:
GREAT
CITY
FOR
A
BEER

MUNICH—Unlike most visitors, I didn't come here for the Olympics. If I want to watch young black men and young white men chasing each other on foot, I can always go south on Chicago's Ashland Av.

Besides, a lot of the foreign judges in the Olympics seem to be putting in the fix. I don't have to leave the Loop to find a crooked judge.

I came here to have a beer. It has become impossible to get good beer in the United States, but this is the beer-drinking capital of the world.

When I told a friend of my intentions, he said a person has to be crazy to go 4,000 miles for a beer. President Nixon sends planes 8,000 miles to drop bombs, and Sen. Hugh Scott thinks the President deserves the Nobel Peace Prize, so I don't feel too crazy.

Besides producing fine beer, Bavarians know how to drink it. They don't pop the top off a can and swill it while watching TV. They gather in huge beer halls, stuff sausages in their mouths, wash them down from giant steins, play table-thumping card games, tell dirty jokes, sing noisy songs, get in fights, and fall asleep with their heads on the tables. They know how to live.

Sociologists have differing views on this kind of activity.

Some say it is beneficial for Bavarians to remain indoors and groggy because that makes them less likely to march across somebody's border.

On the other hand, while they are indoors and groggy, they have been known to be easily inspired by crazy orators who urge them to march across somebody's border.

But that is all in the past, we hope, so let us talk instead about beer.

First, there is the beer itself. The Germans have strict and ancient laws on how it is to be made. They know what to do with people who don't make it properly. Unlike our beer, you can drink great quantities without getting a headache, an upset stomach, or strangling on artificial bubbles. The only bad aftereffect ever noted from drinking Munich beer is an urge to enlist.

Then there are the beer halls, which the many breweries of Munich operate. Chicago used to have a few, but now they are gone. Here they thrive, as do the outdoor beer gardens and the sidewalk beer cafes. Anywhere you look in Munich, you will see people lifting heavy beer steins. They like regular exercise.

Inside the beer halls are rows of picnic benches, brass bands, enormous barrels, enormous waitresses, and enormous customers. The average Bavarian's waistline is about 48 inches. Her husband's might be even bigger.

The king of Munich's beer halls—and my destination—is the venerable Hofbrau House. The main beer room on the first floor looks bigger than a couple of gymnasiums. In fact, when I walked in it sounded as if a basketball game was in progress, with everybody shouting and cheering. As far as I could tell, they were cheering themselves for being drunk.

Seconds after I sat down, a waitress put a stein in front of me. It contained one liter, which is more than a quart, and it's as short a beer as you can get.

Some people were playing an unusual game. First, they slapped themselves rhythmically on the arms and thighs. Then they slapped each other in the face. The purpose of the game appeared to be to keep each other awake so they could drink more.

Everybody was eating, drinking, singing, or slapping. A few were doing all at the same time.

Then a young American got up and walked unsteadily toward the door.

He was about 22, tall, broad-shouldered, wearing jeans, an undershirt, and carrying a backpack with one arm. His other hand was behind him because he was trying to conceal one of the beer steins.

Stealing a beer stein is a criminal offense, because they sell them as souvenirs. They even have a sign posted saying it is against the law to steal a beer stein. In most places, stealing anything is a crime. Here, the theft of a beer stein is a special crime.

He didn't make it. Just as he got to the door, a sharp-eyed waitress supervisor spotted him, slammed down her stein, wiped the foam off her chin, and jumped up.

She looked like something out of "Cabaret." If you can, picture a pink-skinned Missouri porker, standing on its hind legs and wearing a yellow wig, red lipstick, tight sweater, and miniskirt.

"Giff me dot," she bellowed, yanking the stein from his hand.

"I paid for that," he said, trying to grab it back.

But she danced away with it, while yelling: "Hey, you sink vee Chermans are dumb, you lousy mudder—." She spoke pretty good English, I thought.

The young American didn't give up, although a friend tried to pull him away.

"All the beer I bought, I ought to get that free," he said, making another grab.

A short, thin young man stepped between them and gave the American a shove. "Out mit you," he said.

He was a bouncer, despite his size. The bouncers are probably the only people in the beer halls who don't drink much, so they don't expand.

The American shoved back. And out of the bouncer's pocket came a long, black, rubber hose.

It wasn't the kind of thick, heavy hose our cops used in seeking truth and knowledge. His was thin, almost spaghetti-like in flexibility.

The little bouncer began skipping about, swinging it at the young man's head. The American kept lunging and shouting: "Give me the mug." And the bouncer yelled: "I'll giff you ziss," and whacked him on the head some more.

The nearby beer drinkers took a sporting interest, many of them shouting encouragement to the bouncer. Their cheers indicated his name was Max.

I decided to cheer for my countryman. "Grab the hose, kid," I yelled.

The fat woman turned and glared at me.

"Hit him again, Max," I yelled. After all, I was a guest.

It was a standoff for a while. The American didn't land any blows, but Max's thin hose didn't bother him much, and Max's arm was tiring.

Then the fat waitress butted in. Literally. She butted the American with the most prominent part of her body— both of them—and threw him off balance.

This gave Max a chance to plant his feet and swing hard. The hose broke in two and the American staggered out the door, banged his head against a display window, cracked the glass, and stumbled around the corner.

Max the bouncer got a big cheer, and the fat waitress was so pleased she treated herself to two fast shots of schnapps.

But a couple of minutes later, the American walked in again. I began flinching for him.

"I left my sack," he told the waitress.

"Ja," she said, handing it to him.

He turned to leave. Then he stopped and asked: "How much are the steins?"

"Twenty marks," she said.

"I'll take one," he said.

"Goot," she said, smiling and whacking him on the back. "Dot's the vey."

Everybody looked happy. The spirit of the Olympics is wonderful.

ROME: FOCUS IS ON ANATOMY

ROME—"Bella, bella," the lean, young man groaned, as he gazed adoringly at the hips of the woman walking ahead of him on the crowded sidewalk.

Another woman approached from the other direction and his eyes shifted to her chest, her hips, her legs, and finally to her face.

"Bella, bella," he exulted.

He was about 5-10 and weighed maybe 150 pounds. His purple shirt had a long, flowing collar and was open to his navel. A medal dangled against his bare chest, and his black pants were skin tight, flared at his bare ankles.

In his left hand was a man's purse. He had to carry his belongings in his purse because his pants were so tight that even one coin would have bulged like a growth.

For a moment he was gripped by indecision. He looked quickly from woman to woman, buttock to breast, trying to decide which to follow.

He settled on the buttocks and drifted behind them, his head cocked to one side, his eyes unwavering, while he moaned: "Bella, bella."

If a man acted that way in Chicago or almost any other American city, he'd probably be run in for questioning about unsolved sex crimes. The least that would happen is that one of Bella Abzug's followers would kick the hell out of him.

But in Rome he is hardly noticed. That's the way most of the men act. They are probably the city's most interesting spectacle.

If you sit at an outdoor cafe, you watch an endless series of miniature parades.

First comes a woman. She doesn't have to be good-looking, just sound of limb. Behind her will be at least one Italian male, an intense expression on his face.

If she's pretty, there might be two or three of them, studying her like judges at a livestock exhibition.

And if she is exceptionally attractive, a small mob will form, all of them crying out their admiration for various parts of her anatomy.

I asked an American who has lived in Rome for many years why they behave this way.

He said: "My theory is that they have seen so many American movies in which Italian men are lovers, that they feel obligated to do it. I suspect that most of them would prefer to stay home and eat pasta and get fat."

The only time they let up is in the morning, when the workday begins.

I took a walk through the commercial section of Rome at 8:45 a.m. and I have never seen a more listless rush hour.

In any American city at that time of day, you'll see scowls, puffy eyes, grim lips, as people face another day of lying, cheating, and otherwise earning a living.

But along State St., 5th Ave., and Market St., you'll also see a briskness, a bustle, as people stride purposefully toward their jobs.

Not in Rome. At this time of day, most Italian men seem grief-stricken, dazed, disconsolate. Their purses seem heavy in their hands.

Their inner pain is obvious at having to spend a few hours working rather than slinking about crying, "Bella, bella."

I saw one man pause for a traffic light. A buxom girl approached. His eyes made it from her ankles to her hips. For a moment his face brightened and his lips began to move. Then he just shrugged and his shoulders slumped. That early in the day it couldn't be done.

But by nightfall, they are alive again, loping along like a bunch of swarthy, young Groucho Marxes.

Surprisingly, Italian women are a sharp contrast to the men. Despite the fame of Sophia Loren and Gina Lollobrigida, most of them dress as if they are on their way for a Saturday morning at the A&P.

It's not uncommon to see an Italian woman, pregnant and in a housedress, walking with a husband who looks as if he were dressed by Gucci, Pucci, Hoochie, and Coochie.

For every woman's clothing store, there seem to be three or four for men. And the things they sell—I almost blush.

I went in one to get some socks and shorts.

The socks were all right, but then the man brought out a box and opened it.

"I said I wanted shorts," I told him.

"These are shorts," he said.

"I meant men's shorts," I said.

He looked confused. "These are men's shorts. They're very popular."

They were cut in a bikini style. They were a sort of gold color.

And they were made of velvet.

Now I know why Italy gets in few wars, and extricates itself quickly from those it does enter. There is only one Gucci and one Pucci. And you need more than two supply sergeants in any army.

PARIS: HOW TO SUAVE 'EM

PARIS—The moment you walk through the doors of Maxim's, the world's most famous restaurant, they begin sizing you up.

The dignified maitre d' takes in your suit, shoes, haircut, and—most important—your general bearing. All of it adds up to whether you are the kind of suave, worldly person who is accustomed to dining in such a place.

I decided to be as suave as possible.

"Hiya," I said.

He winced. I guess I was too suave for him.

He led me to a table and turned me over to the

headwaiter, a plump man with heavy eyelids and a built-in sneer. He, too, began sizing me up. I sneered back. For a moment it was a standoff, so I blew smoke in his face.

"Would you like an aperitif?" he asked.

"No," I said, "but I'd like a drink."

He sighed and called for the wine steward, I ordered a scotch, a bottle of water, a bucket of ice, and a glass.

"Look," I whispered to him. "I'm not planning on a bender. I want one drink."

He didn't speak English and I don't speak French, so we used sign language, and he took the whole thing away.

The headwaiter came back and said:

"You did not want the scotch?"

"Sure I did, but I don't want to buy a whole bottle. Not before dinner."

His sneer increased. "He was going to pour you only one drink," he said.

"Why didn't he say so?" I said.

He shook his head and sent the wine man back.

The drink gave me time to study the menu, which wasn't easy. In order to appear suave, I concealed my French-English menu translator on my lap.

I'd look at the menu, then at my lap. Then I'd look at the menu, then down at my lap.

I glanced around and noticed a couple of people staring at me. They probably thought I was dozing off, which would be a suave thing to do.

I was only halfway through the list of soups when the headwaiter appeared.

"I'll take that," I said, pointing to a soup, "and that," pointing to a meat course.

He jotted my order.

"And please make it rare," I said.

"Rare?" he said.

"Yes, I like beef rare."

"That is lamb," he said.

"Well," I said quickly, "I like lamb rare, too."

He left and the wine man reappeared, handing me a very long wine list.

I looked for something cheap. The cheapest bottle was mineral water, and that wasn't cheap.

So I looked for something familiar.

I found it. It was the exact same wine I had five years ago in the Sangamo Club in Springfield, Ill., a popular dining place for Chicago and Downstate politicians. They go there whenever they can find a lobbyist to pick up the tab.

That night in Springfield the wine cost $4.

But in Maxim's, only 300 miles from where it is produced and bottled, it cost $30. Where are the lobbyists when you really need them?

I considered the moral aspects of ordering a bottle of wine that cost $30. Is it right for one person to order something that expensive when so many thousands of men on Skid Row are thirsty?

Of course not. But I did it anyway.

He brought the wine, poured a few drops in a glass, and waited for me to approve or disapprove.

That is the moment of ultimate suave. I put my nose in the glass, inhaled, sipped, rolled my eyes, swallowed.

He waited, the bottle poised.

I pursed my lips for a moment, squinted, nodded, and said: "It ain't Welch's grape juice."

He left the wine, and somebody else brought me the soup. When I finished, still another man took the empty soup plate away.

I added them up. Beginning with the maitre d', plus the man who took the food order, the wine man, the waiter, and the man who took the plate away, that was five people. Five people to get me to a table and feed me a shot of whisky and a bowl of soup.

With the chef, it came to six people.

My mother used to handle the whole thing. And she'd still find time to ask me if I was ever going to amount to anything.

They brought the main course. The lamb was mostly fat, but the sauce was pretty good, so I ate the sauce and left the lamb.

The headwaiter noticed that, and he inquired: "You did not like it?"

"It was fine," I said suavely. "But I always eat only the sauce. I'm a vegetarian."

He began looking confused. My suave was defeating him.

For dessert, it was some berries mixed with whipped cream. The waiter waited until I tried it, and then he asked for my reaction.

"Not bad," I said. "But have you ever had whipped cream at The Buffalo?"

"Buff-alow?"

"Pulaski and Irving, in Chicago. Greeks run it. They know how to make sundaes. Try it sometime."

He looked a little dazed. They're not used to somebody really worldly.

The final test of the suave diner at Maxim's is to look at the check and pay it without flinching. I did it. It was easy, because I still hadn't figured out how many francs there are to a dollar. Hours later, when I added it up, I wept uncontrollably.

As I stood to leave, the headwaiter was standing nearby. He had stopped sneering. In fact, he had a pleasant expression of anticipation on his face.

I walked over to him and put out my hand. He put his out eagerly. I gave him a hearty—but empty-handed—shake. Now, at last, he really had something to sneer about.

A "RUMBLE" IN BAVARIA

September 11, 1972

OBERAMMERGAU—This Bavarian village, someone advised me, was the perfect place to escape from the worries of the world.

It was said to be even more restful than a vacation resort, because at a resort there are things to do, such as swimming and golf. Here there is nothing to do.

The big excitement occurs every 10 years when the residents present the Passion Play. But the next performance isn't due until 1980, so the natives spend most of their time carving wood into dolls, statues, religious figures and drunken fat men.

For a visitor, there isn't much to do except sit around and watch the wood shavings land on the floor.

Two hours after checking into a hotel, I had seen all of the sights—some of them twice—eaten a schnitzel, and was ready to turn in.

Then, in the stillness of the night, I heard a sound I have learned to hate—the rumble of motorcycles.

Actually I don't hate all motorcycles. Only those that rumble outside my window at night. I don't mind when they go roaring down a highway at breakneck speeds, because I know there is a chance they will break their necks.

I leaned out the window. On the sidewalk below were half a dozen long-haired young men. They had parked their machines on the sidewalk next to the hotel and were sitting and talking.

I dug out my German-English dictionary and started to work out how to say: "Hey, punks, get the hell out of here before I call the cops."

But then I heard louder voices.

Several elderly men—wearing the traditional Alpine short pants and walking shoes—had come out of their homes and were waving their fingers at the young men.

The cyclists were slouching, hands on hips, and cigarets in the corners of their mouths, like a bunch of blue-eyed, blond Marlon Brandos in a scene from "Der Vild Vuns."

From their expressions and the tones of their voices, I got the feeling that this was a long-simmering dispute.

The old men didn't get anywhere, so they stomped away, and the young men resumed sitting on the sidewalk talking, smoking, laughing, and other things that get old men mad.

But in a few minutes the old men returned and this time they weren't alone.

One of them brought as big and mean a German shepherd as I have ever seen outside a Chicago tavern.

He had him on a long, heavy chain, which he held

with both hands. He gave one command and the dog began howling and gnashing his teeth, straining to get at the motorcyclists.

The young men jumped up and one of them yelled something in German, which I imagine meant: "Hey, are you crazy? That dog'll bite!"

And the old men stood behind their dog, gleefully shaking their fingers and saying something I figure meant: "Damn right he will, kid, so you'd better get."

I started looking in my German-English dictionary for "Sic 'em, pooch."

Just then a car pulled up and a man about 35 got out. He wore a white shirt, sleeves rolled up, and a tie.

Both sides seemed to know him. He put his hands on the shoulder of one of the older men and talked for a moment. Then he did the same with one of the young men.

I pegged him for a social worker.

Both sides began loudly telling him about how bad the others were, and he stood there nodding, looking wise and understanding.

I changed my mind and pegged him for a politician.

He obviously was trying to work out some kind of compromise. But then the sound of the siren approached.

German official vehicles have the most hair-raising sirens. Maybe I saw too many 1940s movies, but when I hear that remorseless sound, I get the urge to flee to a hidden room in a cellar.

That's how the young men reacted. They concluded immediately that one of the old men had called the cops, and they began scrambling.

One was so panicky that when he stomped the starter on his motorcycle, it spun out of control, tossing him into the street. The dog lunged and came within an inch of getting his ear.

Another jumped on his machine, lurched forward, and managed to jam himself between a parked car and a wall.

The terrifying sound of the siren was getting closer and louder. The young men were frantically trying to get their motorcycles started. The old men were yelling. The dog was raging.

All this on a dark, stone street in a quaint village where the natives paint big biblical scenes on the outside walls of their gingerbread houses, and carve dolls.

I couldn't make up my mind—pack immediately or wait until morning.

Suddenly, out of the darkness, the siren was right there. Everybody froze.

The vehicle flashed by and was gone. It was an ambulance, not the cops.

But the sound had broken the young cyclists. They righted their bikes, shakily started them, and drove away.

The old men talked for a moment, then they went home.

I decided I liked Oberammergau. It's a place where a Chicagoan won't feel homesick.

MONTE
CARLO
A
REAL
LOSER

MONTE CARLO—The first time I ever gambled, I knew I was a born high roller. We pitched pennies in the schoolyard, and I threw my penny so high it rolled into a sewer.

This led to shooting dice with other pinsetters in the back of the old Congress Bowling Alley on Milwaukee Av. A sly, old wino taught us the rules. He also taught us never to shoot dice with a sly, old wino.

In later years there were the poker games in tavern basements, on footlockers in barracks, on troopships, in press-rooms, even at police headquarters. I developed a poker face that earned me the nickname: "The Twitch."

Then, about 15 years ago, I read *Casino Royale,* a James Bond adventure. After that it was no longer enough to sit across the kitchen table and tell a relative: "I call your nickel and raise a dime."

As all the graying fans of Agent 007 remember, it was in the Casino Royale that Bond took on Le Chiffre, the evil paymaster of the Soviet murder organization SMERSH, in big-stakes cards.

It was in the glittering, luxurious Casino Royale that Bond's steel nerves and gambling instincts finally broke Le Chiffre, delighting the beautiful woman who watched.

The game they played was baccarat, which is similar to American blackjack, except that the perfect score is 9, not 21.

And the magic word in this game is *Banco.* That's what you coolly say to announce that you are gambling against your opponent's entire bankroll, hoping to wipe it out in one hand, as James Bond finally did to Le Chiffre.

From that day on, after I finished the book, the born gambler in me yearned to look across the felt table in the Casino Royale and to calmly say *Banco,* causing the other players to gasp, and my opponent to sweat.

The trouble was there's no such place as Casino Royale. It was a fictional casino.

So I decided to find the closest thing to it.

A few years ago, I visited Las Vegas. Pot bellies in golf shirts at the dice table. Bermuda shorts at the roulette wheel. And vacationing housewives feeding slot machines.

At the Casino Royale, they wore dinner jackets, gowns, and it glittered like a palace.

I left Vegas without betting a dime.

Before coming here, I tried a casino in Paris. The most exciting moment there was when a cross-eyed hooker winked at me.

Then on to the new casino in Nice. It had a touch of

elegance, with a marble staircase and broad windows overlooking the Mediterranean. But most of the gamblers were little old French ladies, some of them knitting between spins of the roulette wheel. You'd have to shout *Banco* into their ears.

So the search for the great baccarat game in its proper setting brought me along the curving coastal road to Monaco, and the famous casino in its city of Monte Carlo.

Before walking from the hotel to the casino, I prepared myself, in much the same way Bond did (page 44, *Casino Royale*):

> *As he tied his thin, double-ended black satin tie, he paused for a moment and examined himself levelly in the mirror.*
>
> *His grey-blue eyes looked calmly back with a hint of ironical inquiry and the short lock of black hair which would never stay in place slowly subsided to form a thick comma above his right eyebrow. With the thin vertical scar down his right cheek, the general effect was faintly piratical.*
>
> *After pocketing a thin sheaf of ten-mille notes, he opened a drawer and took out a light chamois leather holster and slipped it over his left shoulder so that it hung about three inches below his armpit.*
>
> *He then took from another drawer a very flat .25 Beretta automatic, loaded it, put up the safety catch, and dropped it into the shallow pouch of the shoulder holster. He slipped his single-breasted dinner jacket over his heavy silk evening shirt. . . . He felt cool and comfortable.*

I, too, paused for a moment and examined myself levelly in the mirror.

My eyes blinked back through horn-rimmed glasses.

The lightbulb reflected on my receding hairline. A thin scar on the bridge of my nose gave it a pronounced lump.

I pocketed my thin sheaf of American Express travelers checks, and my French-English dictionary, and from a drawer I took a thin metal can and gave myself a squirt under each armpit.

Then I practiced my facial expression for the moment I would say: *Banco.* I tried squinting one eye and smiling coldly. It wasn't quite right, so I tried squinting both eyes. I couldn't see that way, so I decided on one squint.

I slipped my Dr. Scholl arch supports into my shoes, and left for the casino. I was ready.

On the way I practiced saying it. You can say it softly and slowly: "Bahnnnn-koh." Or snap it out: "Bahn-ko." Or nonchalantly, with a high lilt to the first syllable: "BAHNK-oh." I decided on a simple, soft, but terse, "Bahn-koh," as Bond did it. And maybe I would add a slight yawn.

Then it was there—a huge, baroque building, surrounded by gardens, bathed in floodlights.

In the afternoon I paid the small admission fee, then walked toward the entrance to the gaming rooms. I regretted not having had cleats put on my shoes. The clicking would have been a dramatic touch.

A short, swarthy man checked my pass, then pushed open the door, and I went through.

I paused to light a cigaret and to stand there for a moment, coolly letting my gaze sweep the room, sizing it up, appraising the players.

It looked like the kind of place where a couple of crazy, old ladies would live with 100 cats and stacks of old newspapers.

The furnishings were something from a Goodwill store. The chandeliers had as much glitter as a Pixley & Ehlers coffee cup.

Everything was frayed, worn out. I could almost see puffs of dust rising with each footstep.

And the gamblers looked like they had all just stepped off a five-countries-in-two-weeks tour bus. Golf shirts, cloth sneakers, even blue jeans. The only guys in the place wearing ties were the croupiers and bartenders.

Worst of all, there were slot machines. And they worked electronically, so you don't even get any exercise.

At the bar, a woman was complaining because she didn't get a maraschino cherry in her drink. And as a couple pushed past me, the woman was saying: ". . . And after breakfast, remember, we've got to pick up some more color film."

I looked at the size of the bets at one of the roulette tables. I've seen more action at church carnivals on Grand Av.

The famous Monte Carlo Casino is a dump.

On the eay out, I asked the doorman if he knew Mr. Le Chiffre of SMERSH.

"Well, if he shows up," I said, "tell him I'll meet him outside. We can pitch some pennies."

ON
THE
LAM
FROM
LONDON

LONDON—Some of the aunts and uncles say grandpa got on a boat and left the Old Country because of political persecution.

But the way others tell it, he left because he heisted an oxcart full of somebody else's booze and they were after him.

In either case, he was running away from something, as were most immigrants, whether it was unemployment, famine, cops, or the peasant system.

I sometimes wondered how he felt. Now I know.

It was my last full day here. I had decided to rent a car and drive to a small coastal village to visit some friends.

The next morning I would drive to the port, turn in the rented car, and board a ship for my return trip home.

A London friend had said to me: "Are you sure you want to drive a car here? We drive on the opposite side."

I laughed. "If you can drive in Chicago, old chap, you can drive anywhere."

Two minutes after I pulled out of the London rental agency to drive to my hotel and get my luggage, I was lost. And I was squeezing the steering wheel.

I don't care what you have heard about the drivers of Rome or Paris, or how many times you have made it through the Edens-Kennedy whirlpool, or survived the Dan Ryan on a Saturday night. They are Sunday-morning drives compared with London.

Left-side driving is part of it. It's much harder to adjust to than you might think.

But the real terror comes from the London streets and the English driver.

London wasn't laid out for cars. I don't think it was laid out for the horse and carriage. The narrow, winding streets—none of which appears to be more than three blocks long—were designed for Jack the Ripper to prowl in fogs. They are so difficult and complicated that men study the London Street guide for years in order to pass a cab-driving test.

Every Englishman seems to be driving a fast sports car—MGs, Triumphs, Jaguars—racing from lights, skidding around corners. It's like holding a road race in a maze.

And I was in the middle of it, going around and around, up this street, down that street, looking for the hotel.

I would have stopped and asked directions, but as far as I could tell, you are not allowed to park anywhere in

London. Once you start driving, you must keep going until you run out of gas or crash.

As I whirled past Piccadilly Circus for the fifth time, I felt like a 70-year-old Wisconsin farmer driving in Manhattan.

Then it happened. I turned into a quiet, narrow street that had cars parked on both sides.

Suddenly a low-slung car whipped around a corner and came straight at me.

I veered to my left to make room. As he flashed by, there was a loud "whump." Before I could stop, it was followed by a "crunch."

Sweating, I got out. One parked car had a crushed hubcap and a flat tire. The next parked car had a long crease in its side.

The first thought that crossed my muddled mind was: "Call the precinct captain and put in the fix."

But you can't do that in England. It's a terrible thing to be a stranger in a country where you can't get a fair, impartial hearing in the backroom of a ward boss' headquarters.

I decided to find the owners of the damaged cars, confess, and follow the proper legal procedures. I rang the doorbell of the nearest house. Nobody answered. I went to the next house. And the next. Nobody was home.

I looked around for a pay phone to call the police. But they don't have phones on every corner.

The only thing to do was to drive until I found a phone. I drove away.

In two minutes, I was lost again. And I had forgotten to write down the address of the accident. If I did reach the police, I wouldn't be able to tell them where it had occurred.

That settled it. I decided to forget it, find my hotel,

get my luggage, and complete my trip. As for the two dented cars—they could blame their own countrymen for driving like fools.

Then I thought of Maude. Good grief, I could see her. Maude, a plump old Englishwoman, sitting at her window, eating a chocolate, and witnessing the entire affair.

I could see her—the snoopy biddy—watching me get back into my car and driving away from the accident scene.

I could see her writing down my license number, dialing the phone for the police.

I could see one of those matter-of-fact English cops looking in a license-number book, calling the rental agency, and the girl at the rental agency telling him who had the car and where I was going to turn in it.

I could see myself at the port, getting out of the car, holding out the keys to the rental agent. And they step out of a doorway, in trench coats, taking their pipes from their mouths and saying:

"Mr. Royko? I'm Inspector Crichingham from Scotland Yard. We want you, sir. I must warn you that anything you say may be taken down and used against you."

I could see the white-powdered wig on the judge's head and the disbelieving laughter in the rear of the courtroom when I explained, honest, I got lost.

And I could see the gates of Old Bailey Prison swinging open, and the guard saying: "All right, matey, step lively. In you go."

Holy cow, I was a fugitive from Scotland Yard.

That's what I deserved for visiting London with its greasy food. The only reason I went there was to hear Irish jokes. They never tell them in Chicago's City Hall.

Somehow, I managed to find my hotel. As I paid my

bill, the desk clerk looked puzzled. I guess he's not used to guests' hats over their faces.

That night I told my friends: "It's just a small favor, but if someone rings your bell and asks for me, would you mind stalling long enough for me to climb out the bedroom window?"

The next morning I drove to the port and handed the key to the auto-rental agent. He looked startled when I stepped back and put both hands in the air.

But Inspector Crichingham of Scotland Yard didn't appear.

I hurried on board, went to my cabin, locked the door, and stayed there until we were safely outside of the 10-mile limit.

Then I went on deck, looked in the direction of England, and thumbed my nose at Maude.

Another passenger asked what the farewell gesture meant. I told him the story, and ended it by saying: "But I got away—just like my grandpa did."

He nodded. Then he said: "What about Interpol?"

My stomach hurts.

PEEPING TOMS FOR NIXON

October 11, 1972

A press conference was held yesterday to announce the formation of a new group known as "Peeping Toms for Nixon."

The spokesman at the press conference, which was held on a darkened back porch, identified himself as Ernest Stare.

Mr. Stare, who said he is a long-time Peeping Tom, outlined his group's goals and aims. He said:

"This is the first time we have ever rallied behind a candidate because this is the first time we have had anyone we can believe in."

"Peeping Toms, as we are known, have never been in

the mainstream of this society. We have been in the gangways, the alleys, on the fire escapes.

"We have always been viewed with a certain amount of disapproval, suspicion, and disgust. Even the common thief has been treated with more respect.

"Yet, if you look at the statistics, you will find that Peeping Toms are among the least violent of people.

"The few injuries that result from our activities are usually suffered by the peepers themselves, when they tumble out of a tree, fall down a flight of stairs, hit their chins on transoms, or get hit on the head by a closing window.

"Peepers do not steal. They look. They do not embezzle. They look. They do not shoot. They look.

"Despite our proud record, we have long been viewed with contempt. Now, thanks to the Nixon administration, this has all changed.

"The recent Watergate Affair, and subsequent disclosures concerning the Republican Party's activities, have created a new public awareness of peeping, and such closely related activities as bugging, phone tapping, infiltrating, snooping, and general spying.

"For the first time, we have had a leadership that has done something besides talk about peeping—it has gone out and peeped.

"To our delight, these activities have not been viewed with ignorance, anger, suspicion, or disapproval, as would have been the case in the past.

"To the contrary, most people have apparently accepted these acts as being normal behavior.

"This indicates a new, liberal attitude toward peeping, an attitude we welcome and applaud.

"Now, for the first time, I no longer feel like a pervert—I feel like a patriot.

"Because of these developments, we will no longer

stand on the sidelines, or in the gangways. We have decided to come out from behind the bush, to put aside our binoculars, and to take an active role in this campaign."

Mr. Stare was asked how his group hopes to be effective.

"Among other things, we will have a mass distribution of bumper stickers, expressing our views."

The stickers had such slogans as:

"Our Leader Looks."

"Tippecanoe and Peeping Too."

"Remember the Pane!"

"In Your Eyes You Know He's Right."

"Bugging Is Beautiful."

"Support Your Local Peeper."

"Ask Not Who Your Country Can View For You."

"Watch It Or Leave It."

Mr. Stare said he is also hopeful that if elected to four more years, Mr. Nixon will support new laws favored by his group.

"Among the laws we would ask for is one requiring that all keyholes be no smaller than an eyeball.

"We also hope he will recommend that manufacturers of window shades be required to make them of clear plastic.

"And we believe construction companies should make transoms no higher than eye level."

The press conference ended with Mr. Stare and his associates rising and shouting their new political slogan:

"Power to the Peeper."

JACKIE'S DEBUT

A UNIQUE DAY

All that Saturday, the wise men of the neighborhood, who sat in chairs on the sidewalk outside the tavern, had talked about what it would do to baseball.

I hung around and listened because baseball was about the most important thing in the world, and if anything was going to ruin it, I was worried.

Most of the things they said, I didn't understand, although it all sounded terrible. But could one man bring such ruin?

They said he could and he would. And the next day he was going to be in Wrigley Field for the first time, on the same diamond as Hack, Nicholson, Cavarretta, Schmidt, Pafko, and all my other idols.

I had to see Jackie Robinson, the man who was going to somehow wreck everything. So the next day, another kid and I started walking to the ball park early.

We always walked to save the streetcar fare. It was five or six miles, but I felt about baseball the way Abe Lincoln felt about education.

Usually, we could get there just at noon, find a seat in the grandstands, and watch some batting practice. But not that Sunday, May 18, 1947.

By noon, Wrigley Field was almost filled. The crowd outside spilled off the sidewalk and into the streets. Scalpers were asking top dollar for box seats and getting it.

I had never seen anything like it. Not just the size, although it was a new record, more than 47,000. But this was 25 years ago, and in 1947 few blacks were seen in the Loop, much less up on the white North Side at a Cub game.

That day, they came by the thousands, pouring off the northbound Ls and out of their cars.

They didn't wear baseball-game clothes. They had on church clothes and funeral clothes—suits, white shirts, ties, gleaming shoes, and straw hats. I've never seen so many straw hats.

As big as it was, the crowd was orderly. Almost unnaturally so. People didn't jostle each other.

The whites tried to look as if nothing unusual was happening, while the blacks tried to look casual and dignified. So everybody looked slightly ill at ease.

For most, it was probably the first time they had been that close to each other in such great numbers.

We managed to get in, scramble up a ramp, and find a place to stand behind the last row of grandstand seats. Then they shut the gates. No place remained to stand.

Robinson came up in the first inning. I remember the

sound. It wasn't the shrill, teen-age cry you now hear, or an excited gut roar. They applauded, long, rolling applause. A tall, middle-aged black man stood next to me, a smile of almost painful joy on his face, beating his palms together so hard they must have hurt.

When Robinson stepped into the batter's box, it was as if someone had flicked a switch. The place went silent.

He swung at the first pitch and they erupted as if he had knocked it over the wall. But it was only a high foul that dropped into the box seats. I remember thinking it was strange that a foul could make that many people happy. When he struck out, the low moan was genuine.

I've forgotten most of the details of the game, other than that the Dodgers won and Robinson didn't get a hit or do anything special, although he was cheered on every swing and every routine play.

But two things happened I'll never forget. Robinson played first, and early in the game a Cub star hit a grounder and it was a close play.

Just before the Cub reached first, he swerved to his left. And as he got to the bag, he seemed to slam his foot down hard at Robinson's foot.

It was obvious to everyone that he was trying to run into him or spike him. Robinson took the throw and got clear at the last instant.

I was shocked. That Cub, a home-town boy, was my biggest hero. It was not only an unheroic stunt, but it seemed a rude thing to do in front of people who would cheer for a foul ball. I didn't understand why he had done it. It wasn't at all big league.

I didn't know that while the white fans were relatively polite, the Cubs and most other teams kept up a steady stream of racial abuse from the dugout. I thought that all they did down there was talk about how good Wheaties are.

Later in the game, Robinson was up again and he hit

another foul ball. This time it came into the stands low and fast, in our direction. Somebody in the seats grabbed for it, but it caromed off his hand and kept coming. There was a flurry of arms as the ball kept bouncing, and suddenly it was between me and my pal. We both grabbed. I had a baseball.

The two of us stood there examining it and chortling. A genuine, major-league baseball that had actually been gripped and thrown by a Cub pitcher, hit by a Dodger batter. What a possession.

Then I heard the voice say: "Would you consider selling that?"

It was the black man who had applauded so fiercely.

I mumbled something. I didn't want to sell it.

"I'll give you $10 for it," he said.

Ten dollars. I couldn't believe it. I didn't know what $10 could buy because I'd never had that much money. But I knew that a lot of men in the neighborhood considered $60 a week to be good pay.

I handed it to him, and he paid me with ten $1 bills.

When I left the ball park, with that much money in my pocket, I was sure that Jackie Robinson wasn't bad for the game.

Since then, I've regretted a few times that I didn't keep the ball. Or that I hadn't given it to him free. I didn't know, then, how hard he probably had to work for that $10.

But Tuesday I was glad I had sold it to him. And if that man is still around, and has that baseball, I'm sure he thinks it was worth every cent.

SELF-RELIANCE
GOING
ALL
OUT

March 22, 1973

These are exciting times to be an American. After years of self-indulgence, we face the challenge of being rugged individuals.

President Nixon sounded the call when he said: "Ask not what your country can do for you, but what you can do for yourself."

And it was more than talk. Mr. Nixon is showing us the way through his policies and programs, and the public's enthusiasm is appearing everywhere.

People who were drifting aimlessly now have a purposeful gleam in their eyes.

Take Wilbur and Bertha Snapjoints, an elderly couple I know.

275

The other day, I saw them hobbling along the street, after cashing their Social Security check and spending it on a box of oatmeal.

But there was a spry bounce to their limps and a purposeful gleam in their eyes.

"We now have something to do," they wheezed. "For years, we felt useless, just a couple of old fogies sitting around watching our pension check shrink.

"Not anymore. Thanks to Mr. Nixon, we have a new challenge. We found something we can do for ourselves."

They led me into their tiny flat.

"Look at this," Wilbur said, pointing to a stack of medical books.

"After Mr. Nixon said he wanted to cut down on medical care to the aged, we have been reading up.

"Next week I'm going to operate on Bertha's bad hip. Doesn't sound hard at all."

And Bertha said: "When I'm up and around, I'm going to see what I can do about Wilbur's bum leg. If it turns out well, I'm going to send a picture of his leg to Mr. Nixon and ask him to autograph it."

As I left their flat, I noticed two simple, long, pine boxes in the bedroom.

"Made 'em myself," Wilbur said. "We sleep in them with the lids closed. When the time comes, we won't even have to ask for any help with that, too."

What spirit. They should get the ITT Medal.

A little later, I ran into Tuck Poynter, a middle-aged, blue-collar worker. He was on his way home to dinner and invited me to join him.

"Yes," he said, "these are exciting times. Pass the peanut butter fritters."

I told him it was an unusual dish.

"Try it with the broiled bread. We used to eat a lot of

meat, but the little lady told me we couldn't afford it anymore.

"So I turned on TV and one of the President's nutrition experts said we should eat chicken. But that went up, too.

"So the President's diet expert said we should switch to fish, and we did. We even ate the mounted muskie I caught in Wisconsin last year.

"But fish went up. And you know, I haven't felt so invigorated since I fought at Iwo. I sent a telegram to the White House saying: 'Lay it on, Mr. President, I can meet the challenge.'

"That's when I gave my family a pep talk. I said: 'What would John Wayne do in this predicament? Would he just sit there, waiting for someone to do something for him?'

"And my wife said: 'No. He would go out and order a filet mignon because he is a millionaire.'

"Well, that's the way women folk are. But she has the pioneer spirit, and that's when we turned to the peanut butter jar—and we haven't had anything else for weeks.

"Sometimes I think back to the kinds of meals I used to have—steaks, chops, roasts—and I can't understand how I could have been so soft. Damn Democrats. Next year I might even start growing my own peanuts.

"Thanks to Mr. Nixon, every day is a new challenge to my self-reliance, to my ability to do something for myself, to my ability to get my tongue unstuck from the roof of my mouth."

But what if peanut butter goes up?

"I've even thought of that," he said, a purposeful gleam in his eye. "When it happens, we will give up food entirely. The stuff just makes you soft, anyway."

By golly, he deserves the Secretary Butz Medal.

After I left him, I saw Stan Atese, a young veteran, striding briskly up the street, a purposeful gleam in his eye.

"Sure I feel great," he said. "Why shouldn't I? Ever since I got back, I've had something to do every minute."

What?

"Looking for a job. My legs have never been in better shape.

"You know, I used to worry over there. I thought that when I got back something would be handed to me, and I'd lose my spunk, my backbone.

"But when I got back to the ol' housing project, I knew things would be all right. The job-training center was closed, and so was the counseling office. The city lost its summer-job funds, and there's no more money to start a small business. Why, I couldn't even get a slice of apple pie, and the baseball season hasn't started. It felt great to be a vet.

"So I'm getting more self-reliant every day, walking the streets. I don't even care if I find a job, the challenge is so much fun."

But what will you do if you don't find one?"

"That's easy. Stick 'em up!"

He deserves the Military Budget Medal.

A REQUIEM FOR A TAVERN

April 12, 1973

It was 5 o'clock and dusk. In the cocktail lounges along Michigan Av., the martinis were starting to flow. The eager young glands were beginning to congregate in the singles bars on the Near North Side.

But in Swastek's Tavern, 1859 W. Chicago, there were only Stanley the owner, a friend, and the sleeping watch-dog.

Stanley was explaining why, after almost 70 years in his family, the corner tavern was being shut down at the end of the month. A glance down the empty bar would have been enough.

"Just look around the neighborhood. So many of the people are old, living on their pensions. The young people move away as fast as they can afford to. The Puerto Ricans go in their own places. By the time I pay for my license and dram-shop insurance, it costs me almost $2,000. So I think it's time to lock it up."

He took out a copy of an antique-dealers' magazine. "Look, I put an ad in for all my fixtures."

The ad described the bar: 26 feet long, solid mahogany, built by Brunswick in 1886.

Stanley slapped the reddish wood. "When my father opened this place, the bar cost $3,700. That was 70 years ago and you could buy a good brick two-flat for that money in those days.

The back bar was in the ad, too. Also mahogany, with ornate carving, pullout wine racks, and one of those huge mirrors that movie cowboys are always throwing things at.

"Some dealer called me from Kentucky. He said he saw the ad and he was willing to take it off my hands for $1,200.

"I laughed at him. Look at it, the cigar counter, the package cabinet, they're mahogany too. Look at this ancient cash register. It rings up quart, pint, half-pint. You know it wasn't designed for any grocery store. I told him to start talking at $8,000. I don't think he understood what he was getting."

It's too bad history can't be put in an ad because Stanley's fine mahogany bar has had a lot of it spilled across the top.

When John Swastek, his immigrant father, opened the place, a 3-cent-a-ride streetcar clanged past. Men with lunch pails and accents came in after work and ordered their nickel shots and nickel beers. They sat at the tables and played pinochle, banging down the cards until their knuckles were swollen.

"Some people say TV killed the tavern business," Stanley said. "You know what did it? When the police knocked out the sociable card games. People want to do more than just drink in a tavern. Look at the English pubs with their darts."

Or the singles bars, for that matter, with their strenuous games.

In those days, a good tavern was a political center. A candidate could get more votes by buying a round than making a speech. And if he bought enough rounds, he could make a speech and the customers wouldn't even laugh.

Some famous political bellies bellied up to Swastek's mahogany. Mayor William (Big Bill) Thompson came in with the local cigar-puffers. So did Mayor Anton Cermak, an anti-Prohibition hero. Martin Kennelly came around before he was mayor. And one of the regular customers was Steve Kolinowski, the chief deputy coroner. He would thrill customers with accounts of the latest body to be found in a trunk.

The social evil of Prohibition closed a lot of bars, but not Swastek's.

"My father made the proper arrangements with the politicians and we kept operating. We got our beer from the Touhy gang. His driver always wore two pearl-handled pistols strapped to his hips.

"Our biggest problem during Prohibition was Tubbo the cop, remember him?"

Capt. Daniel (Tubbo) Gilbert, a political badge who became known as the world's richest cop. For years he ran the state's attorney's police. And he ran the state's attorney, too.

Tubbo liked to lean on the mahogany bar. But there wasn't a glass in his hand.

"In those days, he was in charge of the district station.

He'd come in here and if we took in $10, he figured his share was $20. No wonder he was the world's richest cop. He could have retired on what he took from us.''

Federal Prohibition agents closed the place once. But that turned out for the best.

''The agent got to talking to my father, and when my father told him about putting his kids through school, and some sickness in the family, the agent said he didn't believe in closing up family joints. He was a family man himself.

''So he not only let us reopen, but he sold my father a load of bonded whisky. Good stuff, too.''

Stanley took over the place in 1937, when his father died. He died right behind the mahogany bar.

It happened the night a young man named Jessie James Jackson came in. He worked in a grocery store, but he pulled one robbery a week. Talk about the work ethic.

''He ordered a bag of peanuts and when my father turned, he said it was a holdup. My father grabbed for a gun in the drawer and Jackson shot him four times.

''Then he headed for the door and my father shot him four times. Then they both fell over dead.''

Stanley has run it since, and until a few years ago, it did its share of business.

But now it is dark outside and the first good cash customer hasn't come in the door.

Stanley looked out the window, at the store on the other corner. It sells junk. ''That used to be a drugstore and it had a running fountain and goldfish swam in it.'' Next to the junk shop was still another junk shop. ''That used to be a real estate agency.'' So on down the street.

He talked about the softball teams his tavern sponsored, the great feasts in the back room when the neighborhood men came back from hunting duck, deer, and picking mushrooms, the kids coming in for a pail of beer for their fathers, the many breweries that used to make beer in Chicago, the three-piece bands—accordian, piano, and drums—that played on Saturday nights.

But he has no complaints, now that it's all over.

"Why should I? Listen, this place was good to us. My father managed to put us all in college. Two of my brothers are doctors and another one is a lawyer. I went, too, but I liked this business. Now my son is a teacher and my daughter is a nurse.

"So I can't complain. This old bar has been good to us."

Solid mahogany, and they don't make them like they used to.

RICHARD, WHAT ELSE IS NEW?

May 1, 1973

I want to be among the first to congratulate President Nixon for his bold new effort to achieve burglary with honor.

If anybody can do it, he can. And he is off to a rousing start.

In his TV speech last night, he began as if he intended to tell us something new about the Watergate Case.

But by the time he ended, we were all marching off together, arm-in-arm with the President, Republicans and Democrats alike, in a crusade to rid political campaigns of any more dirty tricks.

It lacked only Kate Smith and the Mormon Tabernacle Choir belting out a chorus of "God Bless America," and the whole country could have gone to bed with a lump in its throat and a prayer on its lips for the man who is going to lead us to a just and lasting grand jury investigation.

But if anything new came out of the TV report, it could only be that Mr. Nixon added a wistful grin to his stock of on-camera expressions.

Oh, he appeared to have said a few things.

For instance, he accepted the resignations of "Bob" (Haldeman) and "John" (Ehrlichman) and Atty. Gen. Kleindienst.

But when he finished saying what fine fellows they are, their resignations sounded like acts of heroism for which they ought to get medals in a ceremony on the White House lawn.

If you listened closely, you might have heard him accept "responsibility" for the entire mess. At least, for a moment or two, he accepted it.

Lowering his voice, as if trying to sing bass in a quartet, he disdainfully said it would be "cowardly" to blame somebody else.

Then he promptly blamed somebody else, by making a "pledge" that the "guilty" would be brought to justice.

The buck stopped at his desk just long enough for him to pick it up, pose manfully with it, then pass it as far downfield as he could.

Bringing the guilty to justice is no big deal at this point. People were being convicted when Mr. Nixon was still insisting it was a nickel-dime burglary case. And the way they are squealing on each other, more convictions will probably follow.

But Mr. Nixon didn't talk about the kind of "responsibility" that makes the Watergate scandal something to be nervous about: the fact that this crew of lock-pickers made it to positions of vast power in our White House.

In trying to calm our nerves, Mr. Nixon assured us that the "great majority" of people in politics are "honest."

If that is so, then how was he able to so completely defy the law of averages by hiring so many bums?

You would think that somewhere in American politics, he could have found people who thought breaking and entering, bugging, lying, double-dealing, and hush-moneying were pastimes to be avoided.

The least he could have found was one man—just one would have done the job—who was honest enough to tell him what the other bunch of transom-climbers was up to.

But there he sat, telling us that he didn't know what was going on any more than we did. They fooled him, just as they tried to fool the rest of us. He seemed to be telling us—we are all in this together, folks.

The big difference is—he hired them.

But he didn't talk about that. So much for "responsibility." Now you see it, now you don't.

So let us move on to the next trick.

Having told us nothing about Watergate, he switched to matters of great global importance, ticking off awesome chores that await his attention.

Chancellor Brandt is coming to the White House; U.S. and Soviet negotiators and another round of talks: peace in Southeast Asia; inflation, and a better way of life for all Americans.

These larger duties should be claiming his attention, he said, not something as distracting as Watergate.

"I shall now turn my full attention . . . to the larger duties of this office. I owe it to this great office . . . and I owe it to you."

Just thinking about the weight of these "larger duties" would be enough to make ordinary TV viewers sink down past the springs of the sofa.

But hold on. Who was helping Mr. Nixon grapple

with these "larger duties?" That's right. Some of those very same people who are now trotting off to a grand jury.

Mr. Nixon began sliding out of his TV "report" by asking us to join him in ridding politics of foul tricks, an easy enough request to comply with, as most people never bug phones or break into offices, anyway.

He shared with us the dreams he has for this nation: peace, jobs, opportunity, a land where we can dream our dreams and have them, too.

And to use his very words—"decency and civility."

I guess we can never have enough "decency and civility." But I suggest that he save speeches about "decency and civility" for the people he hires. They are the ones in need of it.

BRANDO'S ROLE: A BORING SLOB

There's a scene in "Last Tango in Paris" when Brando talks to his young mattressmate about his unhappy boyhood on a farm.

He had a date, see, and he was all dressed up to take the girl to a basketball game.

But his father, a mean man, told him he had to milk the cow before he left.

So he milked the cow, and because of his father's callousness, he hurried off to his date with cow dung on his shoes.

"I was in a hurry, and I didn't have time to change my shoes," Brando tells the girl. "Later on, it smelled in the car. I can't remember very many good things (about his childhood)."

That is one of the scenes that has prompted some of the nation's best-known critics to rave about "Last Tango" as a great work of art.

But let's stop for just one moment and think about this scene.

There is a middle-aged man, talking about how, many years ago, his mean dad caused him to go on a date with cow dung on his shoes. It is pretty obvious that this experience led to his present condition of cynicism, withdrawal, toughness, sadness, and general indifference to his fellow man. And maybe also his manner with strange young ladies—which includes rape, sodomy, and sexual sadism and masochism.

I have to assume that the cow-dung incident is important, because it is one of the lengthiest speaking parts of the film.

Now, if you were sitting in a tavern and some guy started telling you about how he once was humiliated because he went on a date with cow dung on his shoes, what would you say?

Of course, you would ask: Why didn't you wipe them off, dummy?

How long does it take to wipe off a pair of shoes with a damp cloth? Ten seconds? Twenty? In a minute or two you can even give yourself a pretty good shine.

Once you asked that question, the bore in the tavern would probably shut up, which is what somebody should do if he doesn't have enough sense to wipe cow dung off his shoes.

But here we have a two-hour movie all about just that kind of jerk, and the critics say it is wonderful.

I had gone to a private screening of "Tango" for newsmen expecting to be slightly startled by the now famous sex scenes, but I figured it was worth it to see the rest of the highly acclaimed movie.

As it turned out, the sex scenes—and there aren't many—were the only parts of the film that kept me from dozing off. Take them away, and it is as boring a movie as has ever been made.

Nelson Algren, the great writer, summed it up when the screening ended.

"Why, he's just a slob," Algren said about the Brando character.

That's about it. It is a two-hour movie about a self-pity-ing, self-centered, whining, foul-mouth, boring slob.

And his girl friend has to be the dumbest broad ever put on the screen—a sort of My Friend Irma with her pants off. What can you say about a young lady from a fine family who takes up with the first seedy, middle-aged creep who rapes her?

I don't necessarily object to slobs, or movies about slobs, just so long as they are fascinating slobs, colorful slobs, adventurous slobs, or champion slobs. Henry VIII, for instance, got more and more interesting as his slob-biness increased.

But Brando plays a boring slob. You'll find one or two in every barracks, in every bar, or standing in front of a judge in a police court.

If you'll let him, he'll talk for two hours about why he can't stop drinking, or why he can't live with his wife, or why he can't hold a job. And, when he finishes explaining, he will start right over again.

So what you do is defend yourself by throwing in a word or two of your own: So, it's your liver, drink; or, so quit moaning and divorce her; or, you don't want to work, then be a bum, just pay for your own drinks.

But unless you are a masochist, you don't sit there lis-tening for two hours.

That's what you'll be doing, though, if you put down the $4 or $5 it will cost to see this dud.

The puzzle is why so many critics think it is an outstanding movie, a remarkable breakthrough in cinema art, a film milestone, blah, blah.

I have a theory. Not only about this movie, but about movie critics in general.

Many of them have spent so much of their young lives sitting and watching movies that they haven't been exposed to enough reality.

Movie critics often are people who have been film fanatics since childhood. When their pals were hanging around alleys or getting into fights, they were at a movie. When everybody else in the barracks went to town and got falling-down drunk, they went to a movie.

And when they got jobs on newspapers, instead of looking at dead bodies in the morgue, human tragedy in police stations and courts, and skulduggery in the political arenas, they were reviewing dead bodies, tragedy and skulduggery as presented on a movie screen.

Take Pauline Kael, the most influential critic, whose praise touched off the fame of "Tango." I don't suppose many of her neighbors have been drunken wife-beaters, or that she has spent many days listening to the self-destructive wine-heads from Wilson Av. or Clark St. tell a judge how they got into their mess.

If she had, she would have looked up at Brando and said: "I know him, that's my dog-kicking neighbor Charlie. His wife put him under a $2,000 peace bond."

Miss Kael simply hasn't spent enough time with slobs, that is clear. If she thinks Brando and his dung-covered shoes are so great, she would have had to give five stars to Slats Grobnik's runny nose.

HOW ROBERTO GOT INVOLVED

My idea of a real sports fan is somebody like Roberto Iglesias. He doesn't sit there munching pizza and staring at the TV. He gets involved.

For instance, Roberto got so involved in Tuesday night's White Sox game that he wound up being handcuffed and taken to jail. You may have read about him. He got in a fight with Orlando Cepeda, one of the visiting Red Sox players.

There's never much glory for fans such as Roberto. They run out on the field or fall out of the stands, have a brief moment on TV, and maybe a tiny story appears about their arrests.

292

But they never get to tell what their greatest moment in sports felt like.

So we visited Roberto at a North Side electronics plant, where he has a job packing items in shipping crates. He's 33, married, and has been in this country since he left Cuba about seven years ago.

Roberto said the entire affair was caused by the high temperature of Latin blood, both his own and Cepeda's.

He said the story of his fight, as it appeared in the press, was incorrect. He did not go on the field or into the Red Sox dugout, as was reported. This is the way he says it happened:

"I was sitting by the dugout. That's where I always sit. I go to all the Sox night games. See, I love the Sox. I haven't missed a night game this year.

"Well, in the first inning Cepeda was walking back to the dugout because he didn't get no hit.

"I say to him 'Cepeda, I'm sorry, friend.' He just look at me. He say nothing. He just look.

"See, for any Latin player, I like to see him hit. This is my brother you know? So that's why I told Cepeda I'm sorry he didn't hit, see?

"He didn't get no hit again in the fourth inning. So he came back to the dugout and I tell him again: 'I'm sorry, friend.'

"He say to me—and this is all in Spanish—'Sure, my friend, why don't you shut up, you mother ———'

"So I tell him: 'You don't call me a mother ———, you mother ——— son ————!'

"Then he walk in the dugout.

"He was up again in the sixth. No hit again. I say nothing when he walks back.

"But he stops and looks at me, you know? So I say to him: 'What you want, my friend?'

"He says: 'You are a mother ———, my friend.'

"So I say to him: 'Well, my friend, you are a mother ———, too.'

"Then I say to him: 'If you want anything, I meet you outside.' And he says: 'Well, I'll meet you outside.' "

That's what I mean about a fan who gets involved. There he was, all 5-7, 155 pounds of him, prepared to battle a player who is so burly his nickname is "The Baby Bull."

Roberto resumed his account:

"My blood got hot. You know, Spanish people get high blood pressure. We get excited, you follow me?

"So I go under the stands, down to the men's washroom right by my seats.

"Two kids who was watching me and Cepeda talk, they say to me that Cepeda is in the washroom. So I am walking into the washroom, and Cepeda is walking out of the washroom, and I look at him and he looks at me. It was still the sixth inning, I think.

"Cepeda says to me: 'I want to hit you.'

"I say to him: 'OK, you hit me.'

"So we have a fight, hitting everywhere, in the chest, in the stomach. Then we get locked up together like a dance.

"The ushers come and jump on me and stop the fight and the policemen grab my arm and handcuff me and they take me to the police station.

"I try to tell the big guy chief what happened, but he say: 'You shut up, you mother ———.'

"Then Cepeda come to the police station to sign the papers against me and the big chief pat him on the back and say: 'You all right, my friend?'

"So, now I have to go to the judge, but I have a witness who see the whole thing, and he'll tell the truth, that Cepeda called me the name first, see?"

But what about the next time the Red Sox come to

Chicago? Will this develop into a season-long feud? Will there be a rematch?

"No," says Roberto. "Why should we? He is a good guy."

That's a real sport for you.

PIETY SELDOM WON BALL GAME

May 16, 1973

I've never understood what religion has to do with sports. Why should a coach who leads his football team in a locker room prayer think that a universal deity could have the faintest interest in whether his team can kick, stomp, gouge, bite, and fracture its way to more touchdowns than the opposing leg-breakers.

At some major events, even the fans are asked to rise and join a clergyman in prayers for an event on which millions of dollars is being bet with the nation's bookies.

And now we are getting the pious preachings of a growing band of muscle-flexers called the Fellowship of Christian Athletes.

They keep popping up on TV and in the newspapers, big names from all sports trying to convince us that their spiritual beliefs have something to do with their having achieved stardom.

Then why do some deeply religious men wind up cleaning sewers all their lives, instead of becoming quarterbacks and marrying the homecoming queen?

These young athlete-preachers also talk about the importance of shunning vice—painted women, booze, wild living—while extolling goodness, honesty, purity, thrift, obedience, and kindness.

These virtues, they say, also are factors in their ability to play a game well enough to make $100,000 a year.

Well, I am a sports fan, but I don't see why somebody should preach to us just because he can throw a sweeping curve. And especially when he isn't telling the truth.

The fact is, religion or good character have nothing to do with athletic excellence.

In fact, I would argue that some of the greatest players of all time have been some of the greatest slobs of all times.

With the assistance of Bill Veeck, the flamboyant baseball executive, and George Vass, author and baseball historian, I have put together an All Star Team.

It consists of players who would qualify as members of the Fellowship of Drinking, Brawling, Wenching, and Gambling Athletes.

And I challenge anybody to field a team of goody-goody players who could beat them on the ballfield. Or in the barroom or bedroom, for that matter. My lineup:

LEFT FIELD: You cannot have an all-time team of any kind without Babe Ruth, the home run king. And he is king of this crowd, too. As an admiring Veeck said: "He was a drunk, a braggart, a glutton, a brawler and a tireless lover. He went out to hollywood once to appear in a movie.

The status symbol among movie stars that year was whether they had gone to bed with Ruth. He tried to give them all status." And to think the man still had the energy to play for 21 years, hitting 714 home runs, batting .342, and even win 93 games as a pitcher. You have to wonder how great he might have been if he hadn't wasted all that time playing baseball.

CENTER FIELD: And no team would be complete without Ty Cobb, the all-time batting champ (.367 for 23 years). How important is decency and goodness? Vass says: "Cobb was the meanest, most hate-filled man ever to play the game. And his temperament didn't get any better off the field.

"He would get in knife fights. He once got cut up but he still played the next day."

If only he were around today. I can just hear Jack Brickhouse crying "Hey-hey," as Cobb chases him through the press box with a stiletto.

RIGHT FIELD: It is said that Paul Waner used to sip from a Coke bottle in the dugout. One day, while he was batting, a thirsty new batboy snuck a deep swig. The kid woke up with a terrible hangover. When Waner wasn't hitting the Coke bottle, he hit .333 over 19 years.

FIRST BASE: Yes, I know Hack Wilson was an outfielder, but on my team he plays the infield. He doesn't have to stagger as far between innings.

Veeck recalls: "I walked into the locker room before a game and Wilson was soaking in a tub with three 50 pound blocks of ice. They were trying to get him sober enough to play. He was in terrible shape, but he played. He hit three home runs that day. And in another game, he jumped into the stands and beat up a heckler. He later said he wasn't so much mad at the guy as he was anxious to get arrested so he could get his hangover out of the sun." Wilson still holds the National League record for home runs in a season (56) and runs batted in (196). And for beer steins, too. His favorite bars all provided a one-gallon stein just for him.

SECOND BASE: Rogers Hornsby (lifetime average .358) did not smoke or drink and seldom brawled. So what is he doing on this team? Horses and women, that's what. We do need versatility.

SHORTSTOP: Rabbit Maranville was one of the greatest fielders of them all. Veeck says: "He once staggered out of the team's hotel and got into a fight with a cabbie. He lost. So he picked a fight with the next cabbie and lost. He fought three more of them, and they all beat the hell out of him. So I asked him what he was doing. He said: 'I'm trying to find one I can whip.' " He was still playing at age 42. Had he prayed and drank only buttermilk, he would have probably lasted until he was 41.

THIRD BASE: With Jimmy Foxx (534 home runs, .325 average) you never knew if he was sliding into a base or just falling down. Veeck says: "When he started a restaurant, he showed up for the grand opening four days late."

CATCHER: It was 3 a.m. when Veeck's phone rang. The police in Queens had Rollie Hemsley, the great catcher, in custody for drinking and brawling. Veeck got him out and took him back to the hotel. At about 8 a.m. the police in Brooklyn called. Now they had Hemsley in custody.

Veeck got him to the ballpark, thus depriving Hemsley of a chance to set a new all-time record of being arrested in every New York borough in the same day.

PITCHERS: No pitcher was ever more relaxed than the great Grover Cleveland Alexander when he came in as a relief pitcher during a crucial World Series game with the Yankees. He was so relaxed, he was staggering. But he struck the man out, whether he knew it or not. And when Alexander isn't pitching, we could use the legendary Rube

Waddell. The only things Waddell enjoyed more than throwing shutouts were fishing and drinking. Thus, when he died, they found him in a gin-filled bathtub with three drunken trout.

Who would be manager of this collection of free spirits? Who else but Leo Durocher, whose exemplary habits once got him kicked out of baseball. As their manager, all he'd need would be a corkscrew.

I should caution young ballplayers that I am not recommending that they pattern themselves after the above players. Sure, you might wind up a star, but it is more likely you would slide down the road to degradation and finally wind up as a sportswriter.

ADVERTISING
vs.
FLAVOR

May 22, 1973

When Chicago's only brewery—Meister Brau—closed down
last year, there was some sentimental wringing of bar rags. And
when new owners recently announced that they would reopen it,
a few toasts were raised.

But I don't see what difference it makes, except to the
brewery employes who will get their old jobs back, whether
a beer is made in Chicago or in the land of sky blue water
or in the beer capital of the world.

I have tried them all. I've popped the top and twisted
the cap. I've grabbed for all the gusto I can get. I've said it
all when I've said Bud. I've joined the big beer broth-

erhood. I've not messed around when I'm the one who's got to get the beer.

And regardless of what label or slogan you choose, it all tastes as if the secret brewing process involves running it through a horse.

Oh, there may be a few small, obscure breweries tucked away in remote corners of Wisconsin, making beer that is more than sour-tasting fizz water, but their products don't get to our liquor stores or into the bars. The waitresses don't mention those names in their routine recitations of the available brands.

Our national shame is that we make the world's worst beer! (I'm tired today of Watergate as our national shame.)

In any country of Europe, the flavor means more than the athletic ease with which you can unfurl the pop top. Japan makes good beer, and so does Mexico. Even in wine-loving France and Italy, their beer is excellent. Almost anywhere, the beer actually tastes the way our commercials claim that ours does.

So why not here, where we make more beer than anyone else, and where we have the technological genius to put proteins in our hair and vitamins on our armpits?

Why is our beer so bad that young people are being driven to drinking Apple Dapple wine?

It wasn't always this way. Old men remember when any tavern served a beer with a head as thick as the bartender's.

I can even remember fetching beer in a pail for my elders when I was but a boy, and the swig or two I took was always good.

We made a good beer because the European immigrants had brought their beer-making methods as well as their thirst.

But something happened. Maybe it was Prohibition,

when people like Capone took over the beer business and customers accepted what they got.

Most likely it was the postwar drift to mass production, bigness, mergers, packaging efficiency, and the substitution of advertising for reality.

If you ask the beer industry why our beer is so tasteless, they will tell you that is what Americans want. The industry says it is "light" and "slightly aromatic." I would say it is puny and pumped up with gas. That is why I couldn't write for an ad agency.

I don't know how they can know this is what we want. They haven't asked anybody I know for an opinion.

More likely, they have a mental picture of a typical beer drinker—a top-popping hillbilly who counts his burps and performs the one-hand can-crush as a parlor trick. Or an Archie Bunker who uses it to wash down a potato chip while staring at TV, or as a thumb-sucking substitute, but not as tasty.

I don't believe it is the kind of beer people wanted. It is the kind of beer the industry slowly shifted to making, until most people don't remember or never knew the way it should taste.

It is cheaper to make this kind of beer.

Simplified, we use a kind of barley that is faster to produce and use than that of Europe. And we also use rice or corn, which lowers the cost and speeds up the process even more.

In contrast, Germany's ancient and strict beer-making laws (about the only laws the Germans haven't revoked at one time or another) allow nothing more than barley malt, yeast, hops, and water. Anybody who dared toss even one grain of corn or rice in a vat would be subject to harsh penalties, and would probably be beaten with large steins.

At this point some cost-conscious readers are saying:

Ah, so we do benefit from this awful brew. A better beer would cost more. Thus, we save money. (The reader who says this is probably a wine-drinking wife of a beer-drinker. Why should she care that his taste buds are being abused?)

The answer is no, we do not save money.

You see, the beer industry spends more than $260 million a year for all the ingredients that go into making our faster, lighter, burpier, inferior beer.

But they also spend about $250 million for advertising.

So when you open a can of beer, half your money is paying for the sickly fluid it contains.

And the other half is paying for the ad that convinces you how good it is.

Another round of Apple Dapple, please.

A
MOOCHER
WITH
CLASS

The elderly man on the street corner was very businesslike in his approach.

"May I speak to you please?" he said, in a firm voice.

Without waiting for an answer, he took out a wallet and displayed two identification cards.

They showed that his name was George Fallon and he lived at an address on N. Dearborn.

One of the cards gave him membership in a senior citizens' club. The other showed that he is now 69 years old.

"I am a senior citizen," he said, returning the wallet to his pocket. "And it happens that only a few minutes ago, I was released by the police after posting a bond of $25."

He took out a police department bond receipt.

He didn't look capable of a criminal act. His eyes, behind steel-rimmed spectacles, were clear, his white hair neatly parted. He wore a clean white shirt open at the throat, a dark green knit sweater, and a brown gabardine overcoat.

He appeared to be a kindly old man.

I asked him what he had been arrested for.

"I was picked up in the Loop for panhandling," he said, "Just like I'm doing now."

He held out his hand and, in a pleasant voice, said: "Anything you would care to contribute?"

No hard-luck story. No plea for a cup of coffee or a bowl of soup, or carfare to get to a job or to a welfare office.

It was the most direct panhandle I've ever been in on. Also, the most dignified and tasteful. In fact, I wasn't sure, for a moment, that I was being mooched.

I handed him some loose change.

"Thank you," he said lightly. "Incidentally, the police were very nice. Two of them contributed 65 cents."

Then he nodded good-by, and walked jauntily away, looking for another contributor. With his deft approach, he would probably earn more by nightfall than some of the people who give him money.

I was glad to see that another imaginative panhandler is working the streets. There aren't many really good ones, at least none in the same class as the legendary Greasy Chin Smith, who used to be seen in the Loop almost every day. He was known as Greasy Chin because he gnawed on a long, old bone to dramatize how poor he was.

One of the better ones currently at work is an elderly man who stopped me on State St. one day and, in an urgent voice, said:

"I'm 67 years old and I must go to Minneapolis."

That's all he said. I don't have any idea what it was

supposed to mean, but it sounded so important that I handed him a quarter. I watched him hustle four others before he left for Minneapolis, by way of Elfman's Bar.

Then there is The Weeper, a kid about 12 who operates on the Near North Side and in the Wrigley Building area.

His tear ducts work like windshield washers. When he stops someone and starts blubbering, and the tears flow down his cheeks, it's difficult to figure out what his problem is, except that he needs money.

The Weeper is no two-bit moocher, either. He thinks big, howling that his mother and five little brothers and sisters are stuck at a railroad station and they need $4.90 to get home.

He cornered Studs Terkel on the street one day and was sobbing so hard, Terkel handed him a dollar.

"That's not enough," the kid cried. Studs handed him another dollar.

"That's still not enough," he sobbed, holding both hands to his face. Another dollar.

"Mister, I need more, more," the kid said, tearing at his hair, so great was his grief.

He kept it up until he got Terkel for five dollars.

"I knew he was a moocher," Terkel said, "but what a performance! It was worth twice that much. The kid cried better than June Alyson."

Then there is the kid who works the south half of the Loop. He carries an old charity card with holes in it for coins. He points at his ears to indicate deafness and wiggles his fingers in what is meant to be sign language. If you came up behind him and said "Stickemup," he'd start running, that's how deaf he is.

Some people get mad when they realize they've been taken in by a phony hard-luck story.

Not me. After listening to enough political fund-raising speeches, I find The Weeper almost refreshing.

About

the

Author

Mike Royko is the author of three previous books, *Up Against It, I May Be Wrong, But I Doubt It* and *Boss: Richard J. Daley of Chicago.* In 1972 Mr. Royko was awarded a Pulitzer Prize in the Commentary category, based in large part on the articles in the *Chicago Daily News* that form *Slats Grobnik and Some Other Friends.*